# Single BERLITZ® CASSETTES
## for major languages

## Treat yourself to an hour with Berlitz
### *Just listen and repeat.*

It's fun, not work. And you'll surprise your friends and yourself with the speed you pick up some basic expressions in the foreign language of your choice. These cassettes are recorded in hi-fi with four voices. Bringing native speakers into your home, they permit you to polish your accent and learn the basic phrases before you depart.

With each cassette is a helpful 32-page script, containing pronunciation tips, plus complete text of the dual-language recording.

An ideal companion for your Berlitz phrase book, pocket dictionary or travel guide. Order now!

**$9.95/£5.95 (incl. VAT)**
**use convenient envelope attached.**

## Use this order form and envelope to obtain
## Berlitz Single Cassettes or
## Home Study Courses!

Check the items below that you wish to receive and calculate the amount due in US dollars or pounds sterling. Then add your name and address on the reverse side and complete the instructions.

### BERLITZ SINGLE CASSETTES
$9.95/£5.95 (incl. VAT)

| | | | |
|---|---|---|---|
| Arabic | 218 ☐ | Italian | 206 ☐ |
| Chinese | 221 ☐ | Japanese | 207 ☐ |
| Danish | 200 ☐ | Norwegian | 208 ☐ |
| Dutch | 212 ☐ | Portuguese | 214 ☐ |
| Finnish | 201 ☐ | Russian | 209 ☐ |
| French | 202 ☐ | Serbo-Croatian | 215 ☐ |
| German | 203 ☐ | Spanish (Castil) | 210 ☐ |
| Greek | 204 ☐ | Spanish (Lat Am) | 213 ☐ |
| Hebrew | 205 ☐ | Swedish | 211 ☐ |

**TOTAL SINGLES** ☐

### BASIC HOME STUDY COURSES
$49.95/£29.95 (incl. VAT)

☐ French   ☐ German   ☐ Italian   ☐ Spanish
   86120       86121       86123       86124

**TOTAL COURSES** ☐

Please note the total number of each item requested and complete the reverse side of this order form.

11644

**TO ORDER:**           Please print

**1.** Name_____

Address _____

_____

_____

**2.** Complete the address on the adjoining envelope for either: **Traveller's Shopping Service**

**3490 Lawson Blvd.**     **8, Trident Way**
**Oceanside, N.Y. 11572**     **Southall UB2 5LS**
**U.S.A.**     **Middlesex, U.K.**

**3.** Calculate:

| From New York | From London |
|---|---|
| _____ Singles at | _____ Singles at |
| $ 9.95 each = $ _____ | £ 5.95 each = £ _____ |
| _____ Courses at | _____ Courses at |
| $49.95 each = $ _____ | £ 29.95 each = £ _____ |
| TOTAL  $ _____ | TOTAL  £ _____ |
| (N.Y. residents add sales tax) | (VAT is included.) |

**4.** Indicate method of payment, please:

☐ Check or money order enclosed made payable to Berlitz

☐ American Express ☐ Master Charge

☐ Diners Club ☐ VISA

Credit Card No. _____

Expiration Date _____

Interbank No. _____
(Master Charge Only. Located above your name.)

Signature _____

**Note:** Credit card holders — It's faster ordering by phone. See numbers on reverse side.

**5.** Detach this order form. Insert check or money order in envelope Please allow up to 4 weeks for delivery. (We pay postage.) Order Berlitz travel guides', phrase books and dictionaries through your bookseller.

11644

From: _____

_____

_____

To: **Traveller's Shopping Service**

11644

# Here's what your Berlitz Cassette Course brings you...

1. 90-minute "zero" or beginner's cassette with 10 basic lessons
2. Two 60-minute cassettes — 20 more lessons in all, on what to say when abroad
3. Two illustrated books featuring the text of all cassettes with explanatory notes, instructions for easy reference
4. Unique rotating verb finder showing tenses of all key verbs

There are thirty lively lessons in all — three and one-half hours of playing (and replaying) time. No grammar — not until you're ready. Just listen and repeat at your own pace — in the privacy of your own home.

All for only $49.95 (U.S.A.) or £29.95 (incl. VAT, U.K.) A small price to start you talking like a native! Order now.

# BERLITZ®

# SPANISH
# FOR TRAVELLERS

**By the staff of Editions Berlitz**

Library of Congress Catalog Card Number: 74-1984

Revised edition
17th printing 1983

Printed in Hungary

Editions Berlitz
1, avenue des Jordils
1000 Lausanne 6, Switzerland

# Preface

In preparing this complete revision of *Spanish for Travellers*, we took into consideration a wealth of suggestions received by phrase-book users around the world. As a result, this new edition features:

a) a complete phonetic transcription throughout indicating the pronunciation of all words and phrases you'll need to know on your trip

b) special sections showing the replies your listener might give to you. Just hand him the book and let him point to the appropriate phrase. This is especially practical in certain difficult situations (doctor, garage mechanic, etc.)

c) a complete revision of the section on eating out to make it even more useful in a restaurant.

d) a tipping chart and a more comprehensive reference section in the back of the book.

These are new features. They complement what has become the world's most popular phrase-book series, helping you with:

* all the phrases and supplementary vocabulary you'll need on your trip

* a wide variety of tourist and travel facts, tips and useful information

* audio aids in the form of cassettes, cartridges and LP records

* a logical system of presentation so that you can find the right phrase for the immediate situation

* quick reference through colour coding. The major features of the contents are on the back cover. A complete index is found inside.

These are just a few of the practical advantages. In addition, the book will prove a valuable introduction to life in Spain.

A comprehensive section on eating out will give you translations and explanations for practically anything one would find on a menu in Spain; there's a complete shopping guide that will enable you to obtain virtually anything you want.

Trouble with the car? Turn to the mechanic's manual with its dual-language terms. Feeling ill? Our medical section provides the most rapid communication possible between you and the doctor.

To make the most of *Spanish for Travellers,* we suggest that you start with the "Guide to Pronunciation". Then go on to "Some Basic Expressions". This not only gives you a minimum vocabulary it helps you to pronounce the language.

We are particularly grateful to Mr. Xavier Cañelles and Mr. Philippe Stiner for their help in the preparation of this book, and also to Dr. T.J.A. Bennett for his help in creating the phonetic transcription. Additionally, we wish to thank Iberian Airlines and the Spanish National Tourist Office for their assistance.

We shall be very pleased to receive any comments, criticisms and suggestions that you think may help us in preparing future editions.

Thank you. Have a good trip.

Throughout this book, the symbols illustrated here indicate small sections where phrases have been compiled that your foreign listener might like to say to *you*. If you don't understand him, give him the book and let him point to the phrase in his language. The English translation is just beside it.

# Basic Grammar

Here is the briefest possible outline of some essential features of Spanish grammar.

## Articles

Nouns in Spanish are either masculine or feminine. Articles agree in gender and number with the noun.

1. Definite article (the):

|  | singular |  | plural |
|------|------|------|------|
| masc. | **el tren** | the train | **los trenes** |
| fem. | **la casa** | the house | **las casas** |

2. Indefinite article (a/an):

|  | singular |  | plural |
|------|------|------|------|
| masc. | **un lápiz** | a pencil | **unos lápices** |
| fem. | **una carta** | a letter | **unas cartes** |

## Nouns

1. Most nouns which end in **o** are masculine. Those ending in **a** are generally feminine.

2. Normally, nouns which end in a vowel add **s** to form the plural; nouns ending in a consonant add **es.**

3. To show possession, use the preposition **de** (of).

| | |
|------|------|
| **el fin de la fiesta** | the end of the party |
| **el principió del mes*** | the beginning of the month |
| **las maletas de los viajeros** | the travellers' suitcases |
| **los ojos de las niñas** | the girls' eyes |
| **la habitación de Roberto** | Robert's room |

* (**del** is the contraction of **de** + **el**).

## Adjectives

1. Adjectives agree with the noun in gender and number. Those ending in **o** and **a** form their plural by adding **s.**

| | | |
|------|------|------|
| **amarillo(a)** | yellow | **amarillos(as)** |

GRAMMAR

Most other adjectives form their plurals in the same way as nouns—by adding **s** to a vowel ending and **es** to a consonant ending.

| | |
|---|---|
| **un coche inglés** | an English car |
| **dos coches ingleses** | two English cars |

2. As a rule, the adjective comes after the noun.

3. Possessive adjectives: They agree with the thing possessed, not with the possessor.

| | sing. | plur. |
|---|---|---|
| my | **mi** | **mis** |
| your | **tu** | **tus** |
| his / her / its | **su** | **sus** |
| our | **nuestro(a)** | **nuestros(as)** |
| your | **vuestro(a)** | **vuestros(as)** |
| their | **su** | **sus** |

| | |
|---|---|
| **su hijo** | *his* or *her* son |
| **su habitación** | *his* or *her* or *their* room |
| **sus maletas** | *his* or *her* or *their* suitcases |

4. Comparative and superlative: These are formed by adding **más** (more) or **menos** (less) and **lo más** or **lo menos,** respectively, before the adjective.

| | | | |
|---|---|---|---|
| **alto** | high | **más alto** | **lo más alto** |

## Adverbs

These are formed by adding **-mente** to the feminine form of the adjective (if it differs from the masculine); otherwise to the masculine.

| | | | |
|---|---|---|---|
| **cierto(a)** | sure | **fácil** | easy |
| **ciertamente** | surely | **fácilmente** | easily |

Adjectives are sometimes used as adverbs, e.g., **alto** can mean loud or loudly.

## Possessive pronouns

|  | sing. | plur. |
|---|---|---|
| mine | mío(a) | míos(as) |
| yours (fam. sing.) | tuyo(a) | tuyos(as) |
| your (polite form) | suyo(a) | suyos(as) |
| his / her / its | suyo(a) | suyos(as) |
| our | nuestro(a) | nuestros(as) |
| your (fam. pl.) | vuestro(a) | vuestros(as) |
| their | suyo(a) | suyos(as) |

## Demonstrative pronouns

|  | masc. | fem. | neut. |
|---|---|---|---|
| this | éste | ésta | esto |
| these | éstes | éstas | estos |
| that | ése | ésa | eso |
|  | aquél | aquélla | aquello |
| those | esos | ésas | esos |
|  | aquélles | aquéllas | aquellos |

Eso no me gusta.   I don't like that.

The above forms are also used as demonstrative adjectives, but accents in the masculine and feminine are dropped.

Esos libros no me gustan.   I don't like those books.

## Personal pronouns

|  | subject | direct object | indirect object |
|---|---|---|---|
| I | yo | me | me |
| you | tú | te | te |
| you | usted | lo | se |
| he | él | lo | le |
| she | ella | la | le |
| it | él/ella | lo/la | le |
| we | nosotros(as) | nos | nos |
| you | vosotros(as) | os | os |
|  | ustedes | los | se |
| they | ellos(as) | los | les |

Subject pronouns are generally omitted, except in the polite form (**usted, ustedes**) which corresponds to "you". **Tú** (sing.) and **vosotros** (plur.) are used when talking to relatives, close friends and children and between young people; **usted** and the plural **ustedes** (often abbreviated to **Vd./Vds.**) are used in all other cases.

### Verbs

Here we are concerned only with the infinitive and the present tense.

Learn these two important auxiliary verbs:

| **ser** (to be)* | **haber** (to have) |
|---|---|
| yo **soy** (I am) | yo **he** (I have) |
| tú **eres** (you are) | tú **has** (you have) |
| usted **es** (you are) | usted **ha** (you have) |
| él/ella **es** (he/she is) | él/ella **ha** (he/she has) |
| nosotros **somos** (we are) | nosotros **hemos** (we have) |
| ustedes **son** (you are) | ustedes **han** (you have) |
| ellos/ellas **son** (they are) | ellos/ellas **han** (they have) |

* There are two verbs in Spanish for "to be". **Ser** is used to describe a permanent condition. **Estar** is used to describe location or a temporary condition.

Here are three of the main categories of regular verbs:

| Infinitive | ends in **ar** hablar (to speak) | ends in **er** comer (to eat) | ends in **ir** reir (to laugh) |
|---|---|---|---|
| yo | hablo | como | río |
| tú | hablas | comes | ríes |
| usted | habla | come | ríe |
| él/ella | habla | come | ríe |
| nosotros | hablamos | comemos | reímos |
| vosotros | habláis | coméis | reís |
| ustedes | hablan | comen | ríen |
| ellos/ellas | hablan | comen | ríen |

**Irregular verbs:** As in all languages, these have to be learned. Here are four you will find useful.

| Infinitive | poder (to be able) | ir (to go) | ver (to see) | conocer (to know someone) |
|---|---|---|---|---|
| yo | puedo | voy | veo | conozco |
| tú | puedes | vas | ves | conoces |
| usted | puede | va | ve | conoce |
| él / ella | puede | va | ve | conoce |
| nosotros | podemos | vamos | vemos | conocemos |
| vosotros | podéis | vais | veis | conocéis |
| ustedes | pueden | van | ven | conocen |
| ellos / ellas | pueden | van | ven | conocen |

### Negatives

Negatives are formed by placing **no** before the verb.

**Es nuevo.**   It's new.          **No es nuevo.**   It's not new.

### Questions

In Spanish, questions are often formed by changing the intonation of your voice. Very often, the personal pronoun is left out, both in affirmative sentences and in questions.

**Hablo español.**          I speak Spanish.
**¿Habla español ?**        Do you speak Spanish ?

Note the double question mark used in Spanish.
The same is true of exclamation marks.

**¡Qué tarde se hace !**          How late it's getting !

# Guide to pronunciation

This and the following chapter are intended to make you familiar with the phonetic transcription we devised and to help you get used to the sounds of Spanish.

As a minimum vocabulary for your trip, we've selected a number of basic words and phrases under the title "Some Basic Expressions" (pages 15–21).

### An outline of the spelling and sounds of Spanish

You'll find the pronunciation of the Spanish letters and sounds explained below, as well as the symbols we're using for them in the transcriptions. Note that Spanish has some diacritical letters—letters with special markings—which we don't know in English.

The imitated pronunciation should be read as if it were English except for any special rules set out below. Of course, the sounds of any two languages are never exactly the same; but if you follow carefully the indications supplied here, you'll have no difficulty in reading our transcriptions in such a way as to make yourself understood.

Letters written in bold should be stressed (pronounced louder).

### Consonants

| Letter | Approximate pronunciation | Symbol | Example | |
|---|---|---|---|---|
| f, k, l, m, n, p, t, x, y | as in English | | | |
| b | 1) generally as in English | b | **bueno** | bwaynoa |
| | 2) between vowels, a sound between b and v | bh | be**bi**da | baybheedhah |

| c | 1) before **e** and **i** like **th** in **thin** | th | **centro** | thayntroa |
| | 2) otherwise, like **k** in **kit** | k | **como** | koamoa |
| ch | as in English | ch | **mucho** | moochoa |
| d | 1) generally as in **dog**, although less decisive | d | **donde** | doanday |
| | 2) between vowels and at the end of a word, like **th** in **this** | dh | **edad** | aydhahdh |
| g | 1) before **e** and **i**, like **ch** in Scottish **loch** | kh | **urgente** | oorkhayntay |
| | 2) between vowels and sometimes inside a word, a weak, voiced version of the **ch** in **loch** | g | **agua** | ahgwah |
| | 3) otherwise, like **g** in **go** | g | **ninguno** | neengoonoa |
| h | always silent | | **hombre** | ombray |
| j | like **ch** in Scottish **loch** | kh | **bajo** | bahkhoa |
| ll | like **lli** in **million** | ly | **lleno** | lyaynoa |
| ñ | like **ni** in **onion** | ñ | **señor** | sayñor |
| qu | like **k** in **kit** | k | **quince** | keenthay |
| r | more strongly trilled (like a Scottish **r**), especially at the beginning of a word | r | **río** | reeoa |
| rr | strongly trilled | rr | **arriba** | ahrreebhah |
| s | always like the **s** in **sit**, often with a slight lisp | s / ss | **vista** **cuantos** | beestah kwahntoass |
| v | 1) tends to be like **b** in **bad**, but less tense | b | **viejo** | byaykhoa |
| | 2) between vowels, more like English **v** | bh | **rival** | reebhahl |
| z | like **th** in **thin** | th | **brazo** | brahthoa |

## Vowels

| a | like **ar** in **cart**, but fairly short | ah | **gracias** | grahthyahss |
| e | 1) sometimes like **a** in **late** | ay | **de** | day |
| | 2) less often, like **e** in **get** | eh | **llover** | lyoabhehr |
| i | like **ee** in **feet** | ee | **sí** | see |

| o | 1) like **oa** in b**oa**t, but pronounced without moving tongue or lips | oa | **sopa** | **soa**pah |
| | 2) sometimes like **o** in g**o**t | o | **dos** | doss |
| u | like **oo** in l**oo**t | oo | **una** | **oo**nah |
| y | only a vowel when alone or at the end of a word; like **ee** in f**ee**t | ee | **y** | ee |

**N.B.** 1) In forming diphthongs, **a**, **e**, and **o** are strong vowels, and **i** and **u** (pronounced before a vowel like **y** in **y**es and **w** in **w**as) are weak vowels. This means that in diphthongs the strong vowels are pronounced more strongly than the weak ones. If two weak vowels form a diphthong, the second one is pronounced more strongly.

2) The acute accent (´) is used to indicate a syllable that is stressed, e.g., *río* = **ree**oa.

3) In words ending with a consonant, the last syllable is stressed, e.g., *señor* = say**ñor.**

4) In words ending with a vowel, the next to the last syllable is stressed, e.g., *mañana* = mah**ña**hnah.

PRONUNCIATION

# Some basic expressions

| | | |
|---|---|---|
| Yes. | **Sí.** | see |
| No. | **No.** | noa |
| Please. | **Por favor.** | por fahbhor |
| Thank you. | **Gracias.** | grahthyahss |
| No, thank you. | **No, gracias.** | noa grahthyahss |
| Yes, please. | **Sí, por favor.** | see por fahbhor |
| Thank you very much. | **Muchas gracias.** | moochahss grahthyaco |
| That's all right. | **Está bien.** | aystah byayn |
| You're welcome. | **De nada.** | day nahdhah |

## Greetings

| | | |
|---|---|---|
| Good morning. | **Buenos días.** | bwaynoass deeahss |
| Good afternoon. | **Buenas tardes.** | bwaynahss tahrdayss |
| Good evening. | **Buenas tardes.** | bwaynahss tahrdayss |
| Good night. | **Buenas noches.** | bwaynahss noachayss |
| Good-bye. | **Adiós.** | ahdhyoss |
| See you later. | **Hasta luego.** | ahstah lwaygoa |
| This is Mr.... | **Este es el Señor...** | aystay ayss ayl sayñor |
| This is Mrs.... | **Esta es la Señora...** | aystah ayss lah sayñoarah |
| This is Miss... | **Esta es la Señorita...** | aystah ayss lah sayñoareetah |
| How do you do? | **Encantado de conocerle.** | aynkahntahdhoa day koanoathayrlay |

| How are you? | ¿Cómo está usted? | koamoa aystah oostaydh |
| Very well. And you? | Muy bien. ¿Y usted? | mwee byayn. ee oostaydh |
| How's it going? | ¿Cómo le va? | koamoa lay bah |
| Fine, thanks. And you? | Muy bien, gracias. ¿Y usted? | mwee byayn grahthyass. ee oostaydh |
| Excuse me. (I didn't hear.) | ¿Perdóneme? | payrdoanaymay |
| Excuse me. (May I get past?) | Perdóneme. | payrdoanaymay |
| You're welcome. | Está bien. | aystah byayn |

## Questions

| Where? | ¿Dónde? | doanday |
| Where is...? | ¿Dónde está...? | doanday aystah |
| Where are...? | ¿Dónde están...? | doanday aystahn |
| How? | ¿Cómo? | koamoa |
| How much? | ¿Cuánto? | kwahntoa |
| How many? | ¿Cuántos? | kwahntoass |
| When? | ¿Cuándo? | kwahndoa |
| What? | ¿Qué? | kay |
| Why? | ¿Porqué? | porkay |
| Who? | ¿Quién? | kyayn |
| Which? | ¿Cuál/Cuáles? | kwahl/kwahlayss |
| What do you call this in Spanish? | ¿Cómo se llama esto en español? | koamoa say lyahmah aystoa ayn ayspahñol |
| What do you call that in Spanish? | ¿Cómo se llama eso en español? | koamoa say lyahmah ayssoa ayn ayspahñol |
| What do you call these in Spanish? | ¿Cómo se llaman estos en español? | koamoa say lyahmahn aystoass ayn ayspahñol |

| What do you call those in Spanish? | ¿Cómo se llaman esos en español? | koamoa say lyahmahn ayssoass ayn ayspahñol |
| What does this mean? | ¿Qué quiere decir esto? | kay kyayray daytheer aystoa |
| What does that mean? | ¿Qué quiere decir eso? | kay kyayray daytheer ayssoa |

## Do you speak...?

| Do you speak English? | ¿Habla usted inglés? | ahblah oostaydh eenglayss |
| Is there anyone here who speaks...? | ¿Hay alguien aquí que hable...? | igh ahlgvayn ahkee kay ahblay |
| I don't speak much Spanish. | No hablo mucho español. | noa ahbloa moochoa ayspahñol |
| Could you speak more slowly? | ¿Puede usted hablar más despacio? | pwaydhay oostaydh ahblahr mahss dayspahthyoa |
| Could you repeat that? | ¿Podría usted repetir eso? | poadreeah oostaydh raypayteer ayssoa |
| Please write it down. | Por favor, escríbalo. | por fahbhor ayskreebhahloa |
| Can you translate this for me? | ¿Puede usted traducírmelo? | pwaydhay oostaydh trahdhootheermayloa |
| Can you translate this for us? | ¿Puede usted traducírnoslo? | pwaydhay oostaydh trahdhootheernoasloa |
| Please point to the phrase in the book. | Por favor señale la frase en el libro. | por fahbhor sayñahlay lah frahssay ayn ayl leebroa |
| Just a minute. I'll see if I can find it in this book. | Un momento. Veré si lo puedo encontrar en este libro. | oon moamayntoa. bayray see loa pwaydhoa aynkoantrahr ayn aystay leebroa |
| I understand. | Comprendo. | koamprayndoa |
| I don't understand. | No comprendo. | noa koamprayndoa |
| Do you understand? | ¿Comprende usted? | koampraynday oostaydh |

## Can...?

| Can I have...? | ¿Puede darme...? | pwaydhay dahrmay |
| Can we have...? | ¿Puede darnos...? | pwaydhay dahrnoass |
| Can you show me...? | ¿Puede usted enseñarme...? | pwaydhay oostaydh aynsayñahrmay |
| I can't. | No puedo. | noa pwaydhoa |
| Can you tell me...? | ¿Puede usted decirme...? | pwaydhay oostaydh daytheermay |
| Can you help me? | ¿Puede usted ayudarme? | pwaydhay oostaydh ahyoodharmay |
| Can I help you? | ¿Puedo ayudarle? | pwaydhoa ahyoodharlay |
| Can you direct me to...? | ¿Puede usted indicarme la dirección a...? | pwaydhay oostaydh eendeekahrmay lah deerehkthyon ah |

## Wanting

| I'd like... | Quisiera... | keessyayrah |
| We'd like... | Quisiéramos... | keessyayrahmoass |
| What do you want? | ¿Qué desea usted? | kay dayssehah oostaydh |
| Give me... | Deme... | daymay |
| Give it to me. | Démelo. | daymayloa |
| Bring me... | Tráigame... | trighgahmay |
| Bring it to me. | Tráigamelo. | trighgahmayloa |
| Show me... | Enséñeme... | aynsayñaymay |
| Show it to me. | Enséñemelo. | aynsayñaymayloa |
| I'm hungry. | Tengo hambre. | tayngoa ahmbray |
| I'm thirsty. | Tengo sed. | tayngoa saydh |
| I'm tired. | Estoy cansado. | aystoy kahnsahdhoa |
| I'm lost. | Me he perdido. | may ay payrdeedhoa |

| I'm looking for… | Estoy buscando… | aystoy booskahndoa |
| It's important. | Es importante. | ayss eempoartahntay |
| It's urgent. | Es urgente. | ayss oorkhayntay |
| Hurry up! | ¡Dese prisa! | dayssay preessah |

## It is/There is…

| It is/It's… | Es… | ayss |
| Is it…? | ¿Es…? | ayss |
| It isn't… | No es… | noa ayss |
| Here it is. | Aquí está. | ahkee aystah |
| Here they are. | Aquí están. | ahkee aystahn |
| There it is. | Ahí está. | ahee aystah |
| There they are. | Ahí están. | ahee aystahn |
| There is/There are… | Hay… | igh |
| Is there/Are there…? | ¿Hay…? | igh |
| There isn't/There aren't any… | No hay ninguno | noa igh neengoonoa |

## It's…

| big/small | grande/pequeño | grahnday/paykayñoa |
| quick/slow | rápido/lento | rahpeedhoa/layntoa |
| early/late | temprano/tarde | taymprahnoa/tahrday |
| cheap/expensive | barato/caro | bahrahtoa/kahroa |
| near/far | cerca/lejos | thehrkah/lehkhoss |
| hot/cold | caliente/frío | kahlyayntay/freeoa |
| full/empty | lleno/vacío | lyaynoa/bahtheeoa |
| easy/difficult | fácil/difícil | fahtheel/deefeetheel |
| heavy/light | pesado/ligero | payssahdhoa/leekhayroa |

SOME BASIC EXPRESSIONS

| open/shut | **abierto/cerrado** | ahbhyehrtoa/thehrrahdhoa |
| right/wrong | **correcto/incorrecto** | koarrehktoa/eenkoarrehktoa |
| old/new | **viejo/nuevo** | byaykhoa/nwaybhoa |
| old/young | **viejo/joven** | byaykhoa/khoabhehn |
| next/last | **próximo/último** | proakseemoa/oolteemoa |
| beautiful/ugly | **bonito/feo** | boaneetoa/fehoa |
| free (vacant)/occupied | **libre/ocupado** | leebray/oakoopahdhoa |
| good/bad | **bueno/malo** | bwaynoa/mahloa |
| better/worse | **mejor/peor** | mehkhor/pehor |
| here/there | **aquí/allí** | ahkee/ahlyee |
| now/then | **ahora/entonces** | ahorah/ayntonthayss |

## Quantities

| a little/a lot | **un poco/mucho** | oon poakoa/moochoa |
| much/many | **mucho/muchos** | moochoa/moochoass |
| more than/less than | **más que/menos que** | mahss kay/maynoass kay |
| enough/too | **bastante/demasiado** | bahstahntay/daymahssyahd |
| some | **unos/unas** | oonoass/oonahss |
| any | **alguno/alguna** | ahlgoonoa/ahlgoonah |

## A few prepositions and some more useful words

| at | **a/en** | ah/ayn |
| on | **sobre/en** | soabray/ayn |
| in | **en** | ayn |
| after | **después** | dayspwayss |
| before (time) | **antes** | ahntayss |
| before (place) | **enfrente de** | aynfrayntay day |

| | | |
|---|---|---|
| to | **a/para** | ah/**pah**rah |
| from | **de/desde** | day/**days**day |
| with | **con** | kon |
| without | **sin** | seen |
| inside | **dentro** | **dayn**troa |
| outside | **fuera** | **fway**rah |
| through | **por/a través de** | por/ah tra**bhayss** day |
| towards | **hacia** | **ah**thyah |
| up/upstairs | **arriba** | ah**rree**bha |
| down/downstairs | **abajo** | ah**bhah**khoa |
| until | **hasta** | **ah**stah |
| for | **por/para** | por/**pah**rah |
| during | **durante** | doo**rahn**tay |
| and | **y** | ee |
| or | **o** | oa |
| not | **no** | noa |
| nothing | **nada** | **nah**dah |
| none | **ninguno/ninguna** | neen**goo**noa/neen**goo**nah |
| very | **muy** | mwee |
| too (also) | **también** | tahm**byayn** |
| soon | **pronto** | **proan**toa |
| perhaps | **quizá/tal vez** | kee**thah**/tahl bayth |

# Arrival

You've arrived. Whether you've come by train, ship or plane, you'll have to go through passport and customs formalities. (For car/border control, see page 146.)

There's certain to be somebody around who speaks English. That's why we're making this a brief section. What you really want is to be off to your hotel in the shortest possible time. And here are the steps to get these formalities out of the way quickly.

**Passport control**

Passport controls and entry formalities are usually quickly dealt with.

| | | |
|---|---|---|
| Here's my passport. | **Aquí está mi pasaporte.** | ahkee aystah mee pahssahportay |
| I'll be staying... | **Me quedaré...** | may kaydahray |
| a few days | **unos días** | oonoas deeahss |
| a week | **una semana** | oonah saymahnah |
| two weeks | **dos semanas** | doss saymahnahss |
| a month | **un mes** | oon mayss |
| I don't know yet. | **No lo sé todavía.** | noa loa say toadahbheeah |
| I'm here on holiday. | **Estoy aquí de vacaciones.** | aystoy ahkee day bahkahthyoanayss |
| I'm here on business. | **Estoy aquí de negocios.** | aystoy ahkee day naygothyoass |
| I'm just passing through. | **Estoy sólo de paso.** | aystoy soaloa day pahssoa |

## If things become difficult:

| | | |
|---|---|---|
| I'm sorry, I don't understand. | **Lo siento, no comprendo.** | loa syayntoa noa komprayndoa |
| Is there anyone here who speaks English? | **¿Hay alguien aquí que hable inglés?** | igh ahlgyayn ahkee kay ahblay eenglayss |

## Customs

The chart below shows what you can bring in duty-free.*

| | Cigarettes | Cigars | Tobacco (grams) | Spirits (liquor) (lit.) | Wine (lit.) |
|---|---|---|---|---|---|
| Residents of European countries and Mediterranean countries of Africa and Asia | 200 | or 50 or | 250 | 1 or | 2 |
| All others | 400 | or 100 or | 500 | 1 or | 2 |

At almost all major airports in Europe, an honour system for clearing customs has been adopted. Baggage is often not even opened, although spot checks are a possibility. After collecting your baggage, you've a choice: follow the green arrow if you've nothing to declare. Or leave via a doorway marked with a red arrow if you've items to declare (in excess of those allowed).

ARRIVAL

| articulos para declarar goods to declare | nada que declarar nothing to declare |
|---|---|

| | | |
|---|---|---|
| I've nothing to declare. | **No tengo nada que declarar.** | noa **tayngoa nahdhah** kay dayklah**rahr** |
| I've a... | **Tengo...** | **tayngoa** |
| carton of cigarettes | **un cartón de cigarrillos** | oon kahr**ton** day theegahr-**reel**yoass |
| bottle of whisky | **una botella de whisky** | oonah boa**tayl**yah day **wees**kee |
| bottle of wine | **una botella de vino** | oonah boa**tayl**yah day **bee**noa |
| It's for my personal use. | **Es de mi uso personal.** | ayss day mee **oos**soa pehrsoa**nahl** |

* All allowances subject to change without notice.

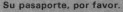

| Su pasaporte, por favor. | Your passport, please. |
| ¿Tiene usted algo que declarar? | Do you have anything to declare? |
| Por favor, abra esta bolsa. | Please open this bag. |
| Tendrá que pagar impuestos sobre esto. | You'll have to pay duty on this. |
| ¿Tiene usted más equipaje? | Do you have any more luggage? |

## Baggage—Porters

You'll find porters to carry your luggage to taxi ranks or bus stops. Major airports have self-service luggage carts which can be found in the baggage claim area.

| Porter! | ¡Mozo! | moathoa |
| Please take these bags. | Por favor, lleve este equipaje. | por fahbhor lyaybhay aystay aykeepahkhay |
| That's mine. | Eso es mío. | ayssoa ayss meeoa |
| That's my luggage. | Ese es mi equipaje. | ayssay ayss mee aykeepahkhay |
| That's my bag / suitcase. | Esa es mi bolsa / maleta. | ayssah ayss mee bolsah / mahlaytah |
| That...one. | Esa... | ayssah |
| big / small | grande / pequeña | grahnday / paykayña |
| blue / brown | azul / marrón | ahthool / mahrron |
| black / plaid | negra / escocés | naygrah / ayskoathayss |
| There's one piece missing. | Falta un bulto. | fahltah oon booltoa |
| Take these bags to the... | Lleve este equipaje... | lyaybhay aystay aykeepahkhay |
| bus | al autobús | ahl owtoabhooss |
| luggage lockers | a la consigna automática | ah lah konseegnah owtoamahteekah |
| taxi | al táxi | ahl tahksee |
| How much is that? | ¿Cuánto es? | kwahntoa ayss |

FOR TIPPING, see inside back-cover

ARRIVAL

## Changing money

You'll find a bank at most airports. If it's closed, don't worry. You'll be able to change money at your hotel.

Full details about money and currency exchange are given on pages 134–136.

| Where's the nearest currency exchange? | ¿Dónde está la oficina de cambio más cercana? | doanday aystah lah oafee-theenah day kahmbyoa mahss thayrkahnah |
| --- | --- | --- |
| Can you change these traveller's cheques (checks)? | ¿Puede cambiarme estos cheques de viajero? | pwaydhay kahmbyahrmay aystoass chaykayss day byahkhayroa |
| I want to change some. | Quiero cambiar... | kyayroa kahmbyahr |
| dollars | dólares | doalahrayss |
| pounds | libras | leebrahss |
| Can you change this into pesetas? | ¿Puede cambiarme esto en pesetas? | pwaydhay kahmbyahrmay aystoa ayn payssaytahss |
| What's the exchange rate? | ¿A cuánto está el cambio? | ah kwahntoa aystah ayl kahmbyoa |

## Directions

| How do I get to...? | ¿Cómo podría ir a...? | koamoa poadreeah eer ah |
| --- | --- | --- |
| Is there a bus into town? | ¿Hay un autobús que va al centro? | igh oon owtoabhooss kay bah ahl thayntroa |
| Where can I get a taxi? | ¿Dónde puedo coger un taxi? | doanday pwaydhoa koakhayr oon tahksee |
| Where can I rent a car? | ¿Dónde puedo alquilar un coche? | doanday pwaydhoa ahlkeelahr oon koachay |

## Hotel reservations

Many terminals have a hotel reservation service or tourist information office. You're sure to find someone there who speaks English.

### Car rental

There are car rental firms at most airports and terminals.
It's highly likely that someone there speaks English. But if
nobody does, try one of the following:

| | | |
|---|---|---|
| I'd like a... | **Quisiera un...** | keessyayrah oon |
| car | **coche** | koachay |
| small car | **coche pequeño** | koachay paykayñoa |
| large car | **coche grande** | koachay grahnday |
| sports car | **coche deportivo** | koachay dayporteebhoa |
| I'd like it for... | **Lo quisiera para...** | loa keessyayrah pahrah |
| a day / 4 days | **un día / 4 días** | oon deeah / 4 deeahss |
| a week / 2 weeks | **una semana / 2 semanas** | oonah saymahnah / 2 saymahnahss |
| What's the charge per...? | **¿Cúanto cobran por...?** | kwahntoa koabrahn por |
| day / week | **día / semana** | deeah / saymahnah |
| Does that include mileage? | **¿Está incluido el kilometraje?** | aystah eenklooeedhoa ayl keeloamaytrahkhay |
| What's the charge per kilometre? | **¿Cuánto cobran por kilómetro?** | kwahntoa koabrahn por keeloamaytroa |
| Is petrol (gasoline) included? | **¿Está incluida la gasolina?** | aystah eenklooeedhah lah gahssoaleenah |
| I want full insurance. | **Quiero un seguro a todo riesgo.** | kyayroa oon saygooroa ah toadhoa ryaysgoa |
| What's the deposit? | **¿Cuál es el depósito?** | kwahl ayss ayl daypoasseetoa |
| I've a credit card. | **Tengo una tarjeta de crédito.** | tayngoa oonah tahrkhaytah day kraydheetoa |
| Here's my driving licence. | **Este es mi permiso de conducir.** | aystay ayss mee pehrmeessoa day kondootheer |

Normally you must be over 21 and hold an international
driving licence. In practice, British, American and European
licences are accepted in almost all situations.

FOR SIGHTSEEING, see page 75

## Taxi

All taxis have meters. The figure displayed at the end of your trip may not be the full price. Legitimate added charges are compounded for night and holiday travel, pickups at railway stations, theatres or bullrings, and for baggage. It's usually best to ask the approximate fare beforehand.

| | | |
|---|---|---|
| Where can I get a taxi? | ¿Dónde puedo coger un taxi? | doanday pwaydhoa koakhehr oon tahksee |
| Please get me a taxi. | Pídame un taxi, por favor. | peedhamay oon tahksee por fahbhor |
| What's the fare to…? | ¿Cuánto es la tarifa a…? | kwahntoa ayss lah tahreefah ah |
| How far is it to…? | ¿Cuánto se tarda a…? | kwahntoa say tahrdah ah |
| Take me to… | Lléveme… | lyaybhaymay |
| this address | a estas señas | ah aystahss sayñahss |
| the airport | al aeropuerto | ahl ahehropwayrto |
| the railway station | a la estación de ferrocarril | ah lah aystahthyon day fehrrokahrreel |
| the town centre | al centro de la ciudad | ahl thayntroa day lah thyoodhahdh |
| the … Hotel | al hotel… | ahl oatehl |
| Turn…at the next corner. | Doble…en la próxima esquina. | doablay…ayn lah prokseemah ayskeenah |
| left | a la izquierda | ah lah eethkyayrdah |
| right | a la derecha | ah lah dayraychah |
| Go straight ahead. | Siga derecho. | seegah dayraychoa |
| Please stop here. | Pare aquí, por favor. | pahray ahkee por fahbhor |
| I'm in a hurry. | Tengo mucha prisa. | tayngoa moochah preessah |
| Could you drive more slowly? | ¿Puede usted ir más despacio? | pwaydhay oostaydh eer mahss dayspahthyoa |
| Could you help me to carry my bags? | ¿Podría ayudarme a llevar mi equipaje? | poadreeah ahyoodhahrmay ah lyaybhahr mee aykeepahkhay |

# Hotel—Other accommodation

Early reservation (and confirmation) is essential in most major tourist centres in the high season. Most towns and arrival points have a tourist information office, and that's the place to go if you're stuck without a room.

The Spanish word *hotel* is pronounced oa**tehl**. There are five official categories for hotels: international-luxury class, first class A, first class B, second class and third class. You may still find price variations within the same category, depending on the location and the facilities offered. There are also, of course, plenty of unclassified hotels where you will find clean, simple accommodation and good food.

Other possibilities of accommodation are:

| | |
|---|---|
| **Pensión** (payn**syon**) | This roughly corresponds to a boarding house. Usually divided into four categories, it offers *pensión completa* (full board) or *media pensión* (half board). Meals are likely to be from a set menu. |
| **Albergue** (ahl**behr**gay) | Modern country inns, catering especially to the motorist. |
| **Parador** (pahrah**dhor**) | Palaces, country houses or castles that have been converted into hotels and are under government supervision. |
| **Refugio** (reh**fook**hyoa) | Small inns in remote and mountainous regions. They're often closed in winter. |
| **Apartamento amueblado** (ahpahrtah-**mayn**toa ahm-**way**blahdhoa) | A furnished flat (apartment) mainly in resorts. Available from specialized travel agents or directly from the landlord (look for the sign *se alquila*—to let, for rent). |
| **Albergue de juventud** (ahl**behr**gay day khoobhehn-**toodh**) | Youth hostel. Foreign tourists wishing to use them should be members of the international Youth Hostels Association. |

HOTEL

FOR CAMPING, see page 90

In this section, we're mainly concerned with the smaller and medium-priced hotels and boarding houses. You'll have no language difficulties in the luxury and first-class hotels where most of the staff speak English.

In the next few pages we consider your requirements—step by step—from arrival to departure. You needn't read through all of it; just turn to the situation that applies.

## Checking in—Reception

| | | |
|---|---|---|
| My name is... | **Mi nombre es...** | mee noambray ayss |
| I've a reservation. | **He hecho una reserva.** | eh aychoa oonah rehssehrbah |
| We've reserved two rooms, a single and a double. | **Hemos reservado dos habitaciones, una sencilla y una doble.** | ehmoass rehssehrbahdhoa doss ahbheetahthyonayss oonah sayntheelyah ee oonah doablay |
| I wrote to you last month. | **Le escribí a usted el mes pasado.** | lay ayskreebhee ah oostaydh ayl mayss pahssahdhoa |
| Here's the confirmation. | **Aquí está la confirmación.** | ahkee aystah lah konfeermahthyon |
| I'd like a... | **Quisiera una...** | keessyayrah oonah |
| single room | **habitación sencilla** | ahbheetahthyon sayntheelyah |
| double room | **habitación doble** | ahbheetahthyon doablay |
| I'd like a room... | **Quisiera una habitación...** | keessyayrah oonah ahbheetahthyon |
| with twin beds | **con dos camas** | kon doss kahmahss |
| with a bath | **con baño** | kon bahñoa |
| with a shower | **con ducha** | kon doochah |
| with a balcony | **con balcón** | kon bahlkon |
| with a view | **con vista** | kon beestah |
| We'd like a room... | **Quisiéramos una habitación...** | keessyayrahmoass oonah ahbheetahthyon |
| in the front | **en la parte delantera** | ayn lah pahrtay daylahntayrah |
| at the back | **en la parte trasera** | ayn lah pahrtay trassayrah |
| facing the sea | **con vista al mar** | kon beestah ahl mahr |
| facing the courtyard | **con vista al patio** | kon beestah ahl pahtyoa |

HOTEL

| It must be quiet. | **Tiene que ser tranquila.** | tyaynay kay sayr trahnkeelah |
| Is there ...? | **¿Hay...?** | igh |
| air conditioning | **aire acondicionado** | ighray ahkondeethyoa-nahdhoa |
| heating | **calefacción** | kahlayfahkthyon |
| a radio/a television in the room | **radio/televisión en la habitación** | rahdhyoa/taylaybheessyon ayn lah ahbheetahthyon |
| laundry / room service | **servicio de lavado/ de habitación** | sehrbeethyoa day lahbhahdhoa / day ahbheetahthyon |
| hot water | **agua caliente** | ahgwah kahlyayntay |
| running water | **agua corriente** | ahgwah korryayntay |
| a private toilet | **water particular** | wahtayr pahrteekoolahr |

## How much?

| What's the price...? | **¿Cuánto cuesta...?** | kwahntoa kwaystah |
| per night / per week | **por noche/por semana** | por noachay / por saymahnah |
| for bed and breakfast | **por dormir y desayunar** | por dormeer ee dayssayoonahr |
| excluding meals | **excluyendo las comidas** | aykslooyayndoa lahss koameedhahss |
| for full board | **por pensión completa** | por paynsyon komplaytah |
| for half board | **por media pensión** | por maydhyah paynsyon |
| Does that include service / breakfast? | **¿Está incluido el servicio/el desayuno?** | aystah eenklooeedhoa ayl sehrbeethyoa / ayl dayssahyoonoa |
| Is tax included? | **¿Están incluidos los impuestos?** | aystahn eenklooeedhoass loss eempwaystoass |
| Is there any reduction for children? | **¿Hay algún descuento para los niños?** | igh ahlgoon dayskwayntoa pahrah loss neeñoass |
| Do you charge for the baby? | **¿Cobran ustedes por el bebé?** | koabrahn oostaydhayss por ayl baybay |
| That's too expensive. | **Eso es demasiado caro.** | ayssoa ayss daymahssyahdhoa kahroa |
| Haven't you anything cheaper? | **¿No tiene usted nada más barato?** | noa tyaynay oostaydh nahdhah mahss bahrahtoa |

FOR NUMBERS, see page 175

HOTEL

## How long?

| | | |
|---|---|---|
| We'll be staying… | **Nos quedaremos…** | noss kaydhahraymoass |
| overnight only | **sólo una noche** | soaloa oonah noachay |
| a few days | **algunos días** | ahlgoonoass deeahss |
| a week (at least) | **una semana (por lo menos)** | oonah saymahnah (por loa maynoass) |
| I don't know yet. | **No lo sé todavía.** | noa loa say toadhahbheeah |

## Decision

| | | |
|---|---|---|
| May I see the room? | **¿Puedo ver la habitación?** | pwaydhoa behr lah ahbheetahthyon |
| No, I don't like it. | **No, no me gusta.** | noa noa may goostah |
| It's too… | **Es demasiado…** | ayss daymahssyahdhoa |
| cold / hot | **fría / caliente** | freeah / kahlyayntay |
| dark / small | **oscura / pequeña** | oskoorah / paykayñah |
| noisy | **ruidosa** | rweedhoassah |
| I asked for a room with a bath. | **Yo había pedido una habitación con baño.** | yoa ahbheeah paydhoedhoa oonah ahbheetahthyon kon bahñoa |
| Do you have anything…? | **¿Tiene usted algo…?** | tyaynay oostaydh ahlgoa |
| better / bigger | **mejor / más grande** | mehkhor / mahss grahnday |
| cheaper | **más barato** | mahss bahrahtoa |
| quieter | **más tranquilo** | mahss trahnkeeloa |
| higher up / lower down | **más arriba / más abajo** | mahss ahrreebhah / mahss ahbhahkhoa |
| Do you have a room with a better view? | **¿Tiene usted una habitación con una vista mejor?** | tyaynay oostaydh oonah ahbheetahthyon kon oonah beestah mehkhor |
| That's fine, I'll take it. | **Muy bien, la tomaré.** | mwee byayn lah toamahray |

## Bills

These are usually paid weekly or upon departure if you stay less than a week. Most hotels offer a reduction for children and infants.

FOR DAYS OF THE WEEK, see page 181

HOTEL

## Tipping

A service charge is normally included in the bill, but you can ask:

Is service included ? **¿Servicio incluido ?** sehrbeethyoa
eenklooeedhoa

Tip the porter when he brings the bags to your room; tip the bellboy if he does any errands for you. Hold other tips till you check out.

## Registration

Upon arrival at a hotel or boarding house you'll be asked to fill in a registration form *(una ficha)*. It asks your name, home address, passport number and further destination. It's almost certain to carry an English translation. If it doesn't, ask the desk-clerk *(portero—*poar**tay**roa*)*:

What does this mean ? **¿Qué quiere decir esto ?** kay **kyay**ray day**theer aystoa**

The desk-clerk will probably ask you for your passport. He may want to keep it for a while, even overnight. Don't worry. You'll get it back. He may want to ask you the following questions:

| | |
|---|---|
| **¿Me deja ver su pasaporte ?** | May I see your passport ? |
| **¿Le importa rellenar esta ficha?** | Would you mind filling in this registration form ? |
| **Firme aquí, por favor.** | Please sign here. |
| **¿Cuánto tiempo va a quedarse ?** | How long will you be staying ? |

What's my room number ? **¿Cuál es el número de mi habitación ?** kwahl ayss ayl **noo**mayroa day mee ahbheetah**thyon**

Will you have our bags sent up ? **¿Puede usted encargarse de que suban nuestro equipaje ?** pwaydhay oostaydh aynkahr**gahr**say day kay **soo**bhahn **nway**stroa aykee**pah**khay

FOR TIPPING, see inside back-cover

## Service, please

| bellboy | botones | boatoanayss |
| maid | camarera | kahmahrayrah |
| manager | director | deerehktoar |
| room service | camarero | kahmahrayroa |
| switchboard operator | telefonista | taylayfoaneestah |

Call the members of the staff *señor* (sir), *señora* (madam), or *señorita* (miss). When calling for service, address the waiter as *camarero* and the waitress as *camarera* since the Spaniards don't make any distinction between the functions of waiter and room service personnel.

## General requirements

| Please ask the maid to come up. | Por favor, dígale a la camarera que suba. | por fahbhor deegahlay ah lah kahmahrayrah kay soobhah |
| Who is it? | ¿Quién es? | kyayn ayss |
| Just a minute. | Un momento. | oon moamayntoa |
| Come in! | ¡Adelante! | ahdhaylahntay |
| Is there a bath on this floor? | ¿Hay baño en este piso? | igh bahñoa ayn aystay peessoa |
| Where's the plug for the shaver? | ¿Dónde está el enchufe para la máquina de afeitar? | doanday aystah ayl aynchoofay pahrah lah mahkeenah day ahfaytahr |
| What's the voltage here? | ¿Cuál es el voltaje aquí? | kwahl ayss ayl boltahkhay ahkee |
| Can we have breakfast in our room? | ¿Podemos desayunar en nuestra habitación? | poadhaymoass dayssahyoonahr ayn nwaystrah ahbheetahthyon |
| I'd like to leave this in your safe. | Me gustaría dejar esto en su caja fuerte. | may goostahreeah daykhahr aystoa ayn soo kahkhah fwehrtay |
| Can you find me a baby-sitter? | ¿Podría buscarme una persona para cuidar a los niños? | poadreeah booskahrmay oonah pehrsoanah pahrah kweedhahr ah loss neeñoass |

HOTEL SERVICE

| May I have a / an / some...? | ¿Me puede dar...? | may **pway**dhay dahr |
|---|---|---|
| ashtray | un cenicero | oon thayneet**hay**roa |
| bath towel | una toalla de baño | oonah toaah**l**yah day **bah**ñoa |
| extra blanket | una manta más | oonah **mahn**tah mahss |
| envelopes | unos sobres | oonoass **soa**brayss |
| (more) hangers | (más) perchas | (mahss) **pehr**chahss |
| ice cubes | cubitos de hielo | koob**hee**toass day **yay**loa |
| extra pillow | una almohada más | oonah ahlmoa**ah**dhah mahss |
| reading-lamp | una lámpara para leer | oonah **lahm**pahrah pahrah **lay**ehr |
| soap | jabón | khah**bhon** |
| writing-paper | papel de escribir | pah**pehl** day ayskree**bheer** |
| Where's the...? | ¿Dónde está...? | **doan**day ay**stah** |
| barber's | la peluquería | lah paylookay**ree**ah |
| bathroom | el cuarto de baño | ayl **kwahr**toa day **bah**ñoa |
| beauty salon | el salón de belleza | ayl sah**lon** day bayl**yay**thah |
| dining-room | el comedor | ayl koama**dhor** |
| hairdresser's | la peluquería | lah paylookay**ree**ah |
| restaurant | el restaurante | ayl raystow**rahn**tay |
| television room | la sala de televisión | lah **sah**lah day taylaybhees**syon** |
| toilet | el servicio | ayl sayr**bee**thyoa |

## Breakfast

The continental breakfast consists of coffee, *bollos* (**boal**-yoass—crisp buns or rolls), *croissants* (**krwah**ssahn—flaky pastry in the shape of a crescent), and *mermelada* (mehrmay-**lah**dhah—usually jam, not marmalade). However, most hotels now provide an English or American breakfast.

| I'll have a / an / some... | Tomaré... | toamah**ray** |
|---|---|---|
| bacon and eggs | huevos con tocino | way**bhoass** kon toa**thee**noa |
| cereal | cereales | thayra**yah**layss |
| hot / cold | calientes / fríos | kahl**yayn**tayss / **free**oass |
| eggs | huevos | way**bhoass** |
| boiled egg | huevo cocido | way**bhoa** koa**thee**dhoa |
| soft | pasado por agua | pah**ssah**dhoa por **ah**gwah |
| medium | blando (mollet) | **blahn**doa (**moal**yayt) |

| | | |
|---|---|---|
| hard | **duro** | dooroa |
| fried eggs | **huevos fritos** | waybhoass freetoass |
| scrambled eggs | **huevos revueltos** | waybhoass raybhwayltoass |
| fruit juice | **un jugo de fruta** | oon koogoa day frootah |
| grapefruit / orange | **pomelo / naranja** | pomayloa / nahrahnkhah |
| ham and eggs | **huevos con jamón** | waybhoass kon khahmon |
| jam | **mermelada** | mehrmaylahdhah |
| marmalade | **mermelada amarga de naranjas** | mehrmaylahdhah ahmahrgah day nahrahnkhahss |
| omelet | **una tortilla** | oonah torteelyah |
| toast | **tostadas** | tostahdhahss |
| May I have some...? | **¿Podría darme...?** | poadreeah dahrmay |
| hot milk | **leche caliente** | laychay kahlyayntay |
| cold milk | **leche fría** | laychay freeah |
| cream / sugar | **crema / azúcar** | kraymah / ahthookahr |
| bread / rolls | **pan / bollos** | pahn / boalyoass |
| butter | **mantequilla** | mahntaykeelyah |
| salt / pepper | **sal / pimienta** | sahl / peemyayntah |
| coffee / tea | **café / té** | kahfay / tay |
| chocolate | **chocolate** | choakoalahtay |
| lemon / honey | **limón / miel** | leemon / myehl |
| hot water | **agua caliente** | ahgwah kahlyayntay |
| Could you bring me a...? | **¿Podría usted traerme...?** | poadreeah oostaydh trahehrmay |
| plate | **un plato** | oon plahtoa |
| glass | **un vaso** | oon bahssoa |
| cup | **una taza** | oonah tahthah |
| knife | **un cuchillo** | oon koocheelyoa |
| fork | **un tenedor** | oon taynaydhor |
| spoon | **una cuchara** | oonah koochahrah |

## Difficulties

| | | |
|---|---|---|
| The...doesn't work. | **...no funciona.** | ...noa foonthyoanah |
| air-conditioner | **el acondicionador de aire** | ayl ahkondeethyoanahdhor day ighray |
| fan | **el ventilador** | ayl baynteelahdhor |
| heating | **la calefacción** | lah kahlayfahkthyon |
| light | **la luz** | lah looth |
| radio | **la radio** | lah rahdhyoa |
| tap | **el grifo** | ayl greefoa |
| toilet | **el water** | ayl wahtayr |
| ventilator | **la aeración** | lah ahayrahthyon |

FOR EATING OUT, see pages 38–64

HOTEL SERVICE

| The wash-basin is clogged. | **El lavabo está atascado.** | ayl lah**bhah**bhoa ay**stah** ahtahs**kah**dhoa |
| The window is jammed. | **La ventana está atrancada.** | lah bayn**tah**nah ay**stah** ahtrahn**kah**dha |
| The blind is stuck. | **La persiana está atrancada.** | lah pehr**syah**nah ay**stah** ahtrahn**kah**dhah |
| These aren't my shoes. | **Estos no son mis zapatos.** | **ay**stoass noa son meess thah**pah**toass |
| This isn't my laundry. | **Esta no es mi ropa.** | **ay**stah noa ayss mee **r**opah |
| There's no hot water. | **No hay agua caliente.** | noa igh **ah**gwah kahl**yayn**tay |
| I've lost my watch. | **He perdido mi reloj.** | ay pehr**dee**dhoa mee reh**lokh** |
| I've left my key in my room. | **He dejado la llave en mi habitación.** | ay deh**khah**dhoa lah **lyah**bhay ayn mee ahbheetah**thyon** |
| The bulb is burnt out. | **La bombilla está fundida.** | lah bom**bee**lyah ay**stah** foon**dee**dhah |
| The...is broken. | **...está roto (rota).** | ...ay**stah r**otoa (**r**otah) |
| lamp | **la lámpara** | lah **lahm**pahrah |
| plug | **el enchufe** | ayl ayn**choo**fay |
| shutter | **el postigo** | ayl pos**tee**goa |
| switch | **el interruptor** | ayl eentehr**roop**tor |
| venetian blind | **la persiana** | lah pehr**syah**nah |
| window shade | **el toldo** | ayl **tol**doa |
| Can you get it repaired? | **¿Puede usted arreglarlo?** | **pway**dhay oos**taydh** ahrreh**glahr**loa |

## Telephone – Mail – Callers

| Can you get me Madrid 123-45-67? | **¿Puede comunicarme con el número 123-45-67 de Madrid?** | **pway**dhay komoonee-**kahr**may kon ayl **noo**mayroa 123-45-67 day mah**dreedh** |
| Do you have any stamps? | **¿Tiene usted sellos?** | **tyay**nay oos**taydh** **say**lyoass |
| Would you please mail this for me? | **Por favor, ¿mandaría usted esto por correo?** | por fah**bhor** mahndah**ree**ah oos**taydh** **ay**stoa por kor**re**hoa |
| Are there any messages for me? | **¿Hay algún recado para mí?** | igh ahl**goon** ray**kah**dhoa **pah**rah mee |

FOR POST OFFICE AND TELEPHONE, see pages 137–141

## Checking out

| | | |
|---|---|---|
| May I please have my bill? | Por favor, ¿puede darme mi cuenta? | por fahbhor pwaydhay dahrmay mee kwayntah |
| I'm leaving early tomorrow. Please have my bill ready. | Me marcho mañana temprano. Por favor, tenga mi cuenta preparada. | may mahrchoa mahñahnah taymprahnoa. por fahbhor tayngah mee kwayntah praypahrahdhah |
| We'll be checking out around noon | Nos marcharemos alrededor del mediodía. | noss mahrchahraymoass ahlrehdhaydhor dayl maydhyoadheeah |
| I must leave at once. | Debo marcharme ahora mismo. | daybhoa mahrchahrmay ahorah meesmoa |
| Is everything included? | ¿Está todo incluido? | aystah toadhoa eenklooeedhoa |
| You've made a mistake in this bill, I think. | Creo que se ha equivocado usted en esta cuenta. | krehoa kay say ah aykeebhoakahdhoa oostaydh ayn aystah kwayntah |
| Can you get us a taxi? | ¿Puede usted avisar un taxi? | pwaydhay oostaydh ahbheesahlir òòn tahksee |
| When's the next...to Barcelona? | ¿A qué hora sale el próximo...para Barcelona? | ah kay oarah sahlay ayl proksseemoa...pahrah bahrthayloanah |
| bus / train / plane | autobús / tren / avión | owtoabhooss / trayn / ahbhyon |
| Would you send someone to bring down our baggage? | ¿Quiere usted mandar a alguien para bajar nuestro equipaje? | kyayray oostaydh mahndahr ah ahlgyayn pahrah bahkhahr nwaystroa aykeepahkhay |
| We're in a great hurry. | Tenemos mucha prisa. | taynaymoss moochah preessah |
| Here's the forwarding address. | Estas son las señas adonde remitir mi correo. | aystahss son lahss sayñahss ahdhoanday rehmeeteer mee korrehoa |
| You have my home address. | Ya tiene usted las señas de mi casa. | yah tyaynay oostaydh lahss sayñahss day mee kahssah |
| It's been a very enjoyable stay. | Ha sido una estancia muy agradable. | ah seedhoa oonah aystahnthyah mwee ahgrahdhahblay |

FOR TAXI, see page 27

HOTEL SERVICE

# Eating out

There are many types of places where you can eat and drink in Spain.

| | |
|---|---|
| **Albergue de carretera** (ahlbehrgay day kahrrehtayrah) | Motel; newly built and strategically located on main roads; snacks and full meals offered, quick service |
| **Bar** (bahr) | Bar; drinks and *tapas* (appetizers) served, sometimes hot beverages, too |
| **Cafetería** (kahfaytayreeah) | Coffee shop; not to be confused with the English word cafeteria; there's counter service or—for a few pesetas extra—you can choose a table. The set menu is often very good. |
| **Fonda** (fondah) | Inn; the food is plentiful and typically Spanish |
| **Hostería** (ostayreeah) | Restaurant; often specializing in regional cooking |
| **Merendero** (mayrayndayroa) | Seaside fish restaurant; you can usually eat out of doors; fine fish dishes |
| **Parador** (pahrahdhor) | An establishment located in a historic castle, palace or former monastery; there are a chain of *paradores* supervised by the Ministry of Trade and Tourism. A *parador* is usually noted for excellent regional dishes served in a dining room with handsome Spanish decor. |
| **Pastelería, confitería** (pahstaylayreeah, konfeetayreeah) | Pastry shop; some serve warm beverages |

| | |
|---|---|
| **Posada**<br>(poa**ssah**dhah) | A humbler version of a *fonda;* although there's nothing fancy about a *posada,* its cooking is usually simple but good |
| **Refugio**<br>(reh**fook**hvoa) | Mountain lodge; menus are simple but food and service are usually of a high standard |
| **Restaurante**<br>(raystow**rahn**tay) | Restaurant; these are classified by the government but the rating has more to do with the number of dishes on the menu than with the quality of cooking |
| **Salón de té**<br>(**sah**lon day tay) | Tea-shop; a bit exclusive |
| **Taberna**<br>(tahb**beh**rnah) | Very much like an English pub or American tavern in atmosphere; always a variety of *tapas* (appetizers) on hand as well as other snacks |

**EATING OUT**

## Meal times

We assume that you've had breakfast at your hotel. See page 34 for a breakfast menu.

Lunch (*el almuerzo*—ayl ahl**mwayr**thoa) is generally served from 1 to 3 p.m.

Dinner (*la cena*—lah **thay**nah) is served far later than at home, seldom before 9 p.m. The Spaniards like to linger over a meal, so service may seem on the leisurely side.

### Eating habits

Most restaurants display a menu outside. Beside the à la carte menu, it'll usually offer one or more set menus (*platos combinados*) or tourist menus *(menús turísticos)* which offer a good meal at a fair price. The service charge *(servicio)* included. A tip is up to you. For a snack you may want to leave some small change, more if you had a good meal. On some set menus you'll notice that wine is included in the price *(vino incluido)*.

Words like *especialidad de la casa* next to a dish listed on the menu are clues that the dish is a speciality of the restaurant.

| | |
|---|---|
| **¿Qué desea?** | What would you like? |
| **Le recomiendo esto.** | I recommend this. |
| **¿Qué desea beber?** | What would you like to drink? |
| **No tenemos...** | We haven't got... |
| **¿Desea...?** | Do you want...? |

### Hungry

| | | |
|---|---|---|
| I'm hungry/I'm thirsty. | **Tengo hambre/ Tengo sed.** | tayngoa ahmbray/ tayngoa saydh |
| Can you recommend a good restaurant? | **¿Puede recomendarme un buen restaurante?** | pwaydhay rehkomayndahrmay oon bwayn raystowrahntay |
| Are there any inexpensive restaurants around here? | **¿Hay restaurantes no muy caros cerca de aquí?** | igh raystowrahntayss noa mwee kahroass thehrkah dav ahkee |

If you want to be sure of getting a table in well-known restaurants, it may be better to telephone in advance. Some of them close one day a week (usually a Monday).

FOR TIPPING, see inside back-cover

| I'd like to reserve a table for 4. | **Quiero reservar una mesa para 4.** | kyayroa rehssayrbahr oonah mayssah pahrah 4 |
| We'll come at 8. | **Vendremos a las 8.** | bayndraymoass ah lahss 8 |

## Asking and ordering

| Good evening, I'd like a table for 3. | **Buenas tardes, quisiera una mesa para 3.** | bwaynahss tahrdayss keessyayrah oonah mayssah pahrah 3 |
| Could we have a table...? | **Nos puede dar una mesa...?** | noss pwaydhay dahr oonah mayssah |
| in the corner | **en el rincón** | ayn ayl reenkon |
| by the window | **al lado de la ventana** | ahl lahdhoa day lah behntahnah |
| outside/on the patio | **fuera/en el patio** | fwayrah/ayn ayl pahtyoa |
| Where are the toilets? | **¿Dónde está el lavabo?** | doanday aystah ayl lahbhahbhoa |
| May I please have the menu? | **¿Puedo ver la carta, por favor?** | pwaydhoa behr lah kahrtah por fahbhor |
| What's this? | **¿Qué es esto?** | kay ayss aystoa |
| Do you have...? | **¿Tienen...?** | tyaynayn |
| a set menu | **platos combinados** | plahtoass koambee-nahdhoass |
| local dishes | **especialidades locales** | ayspaythyahleedhahdhayss loakahlayss |
| Is service included? | **¿Va incluído el servicio?** | bah eenklooeedhoa ayl sehrbeethyoa |
| Can we have (a/an) ..., please? | **¿Puede darnos... por favor?** | pwaydhay dahrnoass... por fahbhor |
| ashtray | **un cenicero** | oon thayneethayroa |
| another chair | **otra silla** | oatrah seelyah |
| glass | **un vaso** | oon bahssoa |
| knife | **un cuchillo** | oon koocheelyoa |
| napkin | **una servilleta** | oonah sehrbeelyaytah |
| plate | **un plato** | oon plahtoa |
| serviette | **una servilleta** | oonah sehrbeelyaytah |
| spoon | **una cuchara** | oonah koochahrah |
| toothpick | **un palillo** | oon pahleelyoa |

EATING OUT

FOR COMPLAINTS, see page 57

| I'd like a/an/some… | Quisiera… | keessyayrah |
|---|---|---|
| aperitif | un aperitivo | oon ahpayreeteebhoa |
| appetizers | unas tapas | oonahss tahpahss |
| beer | una cerveza | oonah thehrbaythah |
| bread | pan | pahn |
| butter | mantequilla | mahntaykeelyah |
| cabbage | repollo | raypoalyoa |
| cheese | queso | kayssoa |
| chips | patatas fritas | pahtahtahss freetahss |
| coffee | un café | oon kahfay |
| dessert | un postre | oon poastray |
| fish | pescado | payskahdhoa |
| french fries | patatas fritas | pahtahtahss freetahss |
| fruit | frutas | frootahss |
| game | carne de caza | kahrnay day kahthah |
| ice-cream | un helado | oon aylahdhoa |
| ketchup | salsa de tomate | sahlsah day toamahtay |
| lemon | limón | leemon |
| lettuce | lechuga | laychoogah |
| meat | carne | kahrnay |
| milk | leche | laychay |
| mineral water | (un) agua mineral | (oon) ahgwah meenayrahl |
| mustard | mostaza | moasthahthah |
| oil | aceite | athaytay |
| olive oil | aceite de oliva | athaytay day oaleebhah |
| pepper | pimienta | peemyayntah |
| potatoes | patatas | pahtahtahss |
| poultry | aves | ahbhayss |
| rice | arroz | ahrroth |
| rolls | panecillos | pahnaytheelyoass |
| salad | una ensalada | oonah aynsahlahdhah |
| salt | sal | sahl |
| sandwich | un bocadillo | oon boakahdheelyoa |
| seafood | mariscos | mahreeskoass |
| seasoning | condimentos | kondeemyayntoass |
| soup | una sopa | oonah soapah |
| spaghetti | espaguetis | ayspahgayteess |
| starter | un entremés | oon ayntraymayss |
| sugar | azúcar | ahthookahr |
| tea | un té | oon tay |
| vegetables | legumbres | laygoombrayss |
| vinegar | vinagre | beenahgray |
| (iced) water | agua (helada) | ahgwah (aylahdhah) |
| wine | vino | beenoa |

EATING OUT

ENTRIES.

## What's on the menu?

Our menu is presented according to courses. Under the headings below you'll find alphabetical lists of dishes that might be offered on a Spanish menu with their English equivalent. You can also show the book to the waiter. If you want some fruit, for instance, show him the appropriate list and let *him* point to what's available. Use pages 41 and 42 for ordering in general.

Here then is our guide to good eating and drinking. Turn to the section you want.

Obviously, you're not going to go through every course. If you've had enough, say:

Nothing more, thanks. **Nada más, gracias.**  nahdhah mahss
grahthyahss

## Appetizers

*Tapas* (appetizers) play an important part in the Spanish meal. Usually they're nibbled on over an aperitif before one goes to dinner. *Tapas* can range from a dish of olives or un-shelled shrimp to marinated squid and vegetable salad.

| | | |
|---|---|---|
| I'd like an appetizer. | **Quisiera unas tapas.** | kee**ssyay**rah **oo**nahss **tah**pahss |
| What do you recommend? | **¿Qué me aconseja?** | kay may ahkon**say**khah |
| **aceitunas (rellenas)** | ahthaytoonahss (ray-lyaynahss) | (stuffed) olives |
| **aguacate** | ahgwah**kah**tay | avocado |
| **alcachofas** | ahlkah**choa**fahss | artichoke |
| **almejas** | ahl**mehk**hahss | clams |
| a la marinera | ah lah mahreenayrah | in paprika sauce |
| **anchoas** | ahn**choa**hss | anchovies |
| **anguila ahumada** | ahn**gee**lah ahoo**mah**dhah | smoked eel |
| **arenque (ahumado)** | ah**rehn**kay (ahoo**mah**dhoa) | (smoked) herring |
| **atún** | ah**toon** | tunny (tuna) |
| **cabeza** | kahb**eh**thah | headcheese |
| de cordero | day koar**day**roa | lamb's |
| de ternera | day teh**rnay**rah | calf's |
| **calamares** | kahlah**mah**rayss | squid |
| a la romana | ah lah **roa**mahnah | deep-fried |
| **callos** | **kah**lyoass | tripe (usually in hot paprika sauce) |
| **caracoles** | kahrah**koa**layss | snails |
| **carne de cangrejo** | **kah**rnay day kahn**greh**khoa | crabmeat |
| **champiñones** | chahmpee**ño**anayss | mushrooms |
| **chorizo** | choa**ree**thoa | hot sausage made of pork, garlic and paprika |
| **cigalas** | thee**gah**lahss | large crayfish |
| **entremeses variados** | ayntray**mayss**ayss bah**ryah**dhoass | assorted appetizers |
| **espárragos (puntas de)** | ays**pah**rrahgoass (**poon**tahss day) | asparagus (tips) |
| **fiambres** | **fyahm**brayss | cold cuts |
| **gambas** | **gahm**bahss | prawns |
| al ajillo | ahl ah**khee**lyoa | with garlic |
| a la plancha | ah lah **plahn**chah | grilled |
| **higaditos de pollo** | eegah**dhee**toass day **poa**llyoa | chicken liver |

| huevos duros | waybhoass dooroass | hard-boiled eggs |
|---|---|---|
| jámon | khahmon | ham |
| en dulce | ayn doolthay | boiled |
| serrano | sayrrahnoa | cured |
| langosta | lahngoastah | spiny lobster |
| langostinos | lahngoasteenoass | crawfish |
| mejillones | mehkheelyoanayss | mussels |
| melón | maylon | melon |
| moluscos | moalooskoass | mussels |
| ostras | oastrahss | oysters |
| palitos de queso | pahleetoass day kayssoa | cheese sticks (straws) |
| pepinillos | paypeeneelyoass | gherkins |
| pepino | paypeenoa | cucumber |
| percebes | pehrthaybhayss | goose barnacles |
| pimientos | peemyayntoass | peppers |
| quisquillas | keeskeelyahss | shrimp |
| rábanos | rahbhanoass | radishes |
| salchichón | sahlcheechon | salami |
| salmón (ahumado) | sahlmon (ahoomahdhoa) | (smoked) salmon |
| sardinas | sahrdeenahss | sardines |
| zumo de fruta | thoomoa day frootah | fruit juice |
| piña/tomate | peeñah / toamahtay | pineapple/tomato |
| pomelo/naranja | poamayloa/nahrahnkhah | grapefruit/orange |

If you feel like something more ambitious try *palitos* (pahlee-toass)—ham, cheese, pâté, smoked anchovy, trout or eel on a skewer. Or perhaps some of these may tempt you:

| | |
|---|---|
| albóndigas<br>(ahlbondeegahss) | spiced meatballs |
| banderillas<br>(bahndayroolyahss) | similar to *palitos* but with gherkins |
| buñuelitos<br>(boonwayleetoass) | small fritters made with ham, fish, egg or a wide variety of other fillings |
| empanadillas<br>(aympahnahdheelyahss) | small savoury pasties stuffed with meat or fish |
| pinochos, pinchitos<br>(peenoachoass, peencheetoass) | grilled mushrooms and kidneys |
| tartaletas<br>(tahrtahlaytahss) | small open tarts with practically any garnish—fish, meat, vegetables, cheese—you can imagine |

EATING OUT

## Salads

| | | |
|---|---|---|
| What salads do you have? | ¿Qué clase de ensaladas tienen? | kayklahssay day aynsahlahdhahss tyaynayn |
| Can you recommend a local speciality? | ¿Puede aconsejarnos una especialidad local? | pwaydhay ahkonsaykhahrnoass oonah ayspaythyahleedhahdh loakahl |

| | | |
|---|---|---|
| ensalada | aynsahlahdhah | salad |
| de gambas | day **gahm**bahss | shrimp |
| de lechuga | day lay**choo**gah | green |
| de patata | day pah**tah**tah | potato |
| de pepino | day pay**pee**noa | cucumber |
| de tomate | day toa**mah**tay | tomato |

## Soups

In Spain, soup is undoubtedly the most popular first course. There is a great variety of soups ranging from the simple *sopa de ajo* to the filling *sopa de mariscos*. Here are a few that you're sure to find on the menu during your trip.

| | | |
|---|---|---|
| cocido (madrileño) | koat**hee**dhoa (mahdreelay**ño**a) | vegetable-meat soup |
| consomé al Jerez | konsoa**may** ahl khay**rayth** | chicken broth with sherry |
| sopa de ajo | **soa**pah day **ahk**hoa | garlic soup |
| sopa de arroz | **soa**pah day ar**roth** | rice soup |
| sopa de cangrejos | **soa**pah day kahn**greh**khoass | crayfish soup |
| sopa de cebolla | **soa**pah day thay**boa**lyah | onion soup |
| sopa de espárragos | **soa**pah day ays**pahr**rahgoass | asparagus soup |
| sopa de fideos | **soa**pah day fee**dhay**oass | noodle soup |
| sopa Juliana | **soa**pah joo**lyah**nah | bouillon of finely shredded vegetables |
| sopa de mariscos | **soa**pah day mah**rees**koass | seafood soup |
| sopa de patatas | **soa**pah day pah**tah**tahss | potato soup |
| sopa de pescado | **soa**pah day pays**kah**dhoa | fish soup |
| sopa de tomate | **soa**pah day toa**mah**tay | tomato soup |
| sopa de tortuga | **soa**pah day tor**too**gah | turtle soup |
| sopa de verduras | **soa**pah day behr**doo**rahss | soup of salad greens |

| | |
|---|---|
| **caldo gallego** (kahldoa gahlyehgoa) | soup of headcheese, spicy pork sausage and vegetables |
| **gazpacho** (gahthpahchoa) | a chilled soup of onion, tomato, green pepper, bread, garlic |

## Egg dishes and omelets

The Spanish omelet is more likely to be round rather than the rolled form of the classic French *omelette*. Here are the names of a few of the more common egg dishes you're likely to find on the menu:

| | |
|---|---|
| **huevos a la flamenca** (waybhoass ah lah flahmaynkah) | eggs baked with tomato, onion and diced ham; often garnished with asparagus tips, red peppers or slices of spicy pork sausage |
| **al nido** (ahl needhoa) | "eggs in the nest"; egg yolks set in small, soft rolls; fried and then covered in egg white |
| **al trote** (ahl troatay) | boiled eggs filled with tunny (tuna) fish and dressed with mayonnaise |
| **revueltos al pisto** (raywayltoass ahl peestoa) | scrambled eggs with vegetables |

| tortilla | toarteelyah | omelet |
|---|---|---|
| **de alcachofa** | day ahlkahchoafah | artichoke omelet |
| **de cebolla** | day thayboalyah | onion omelet |
| **de espárragos** | day ayspahrrahgoass | asparagus omelet |
| **gallega** | gahlyehgah | potato omelet with ham, chili peppers and peas |
| **de jamón** | day khamon | ham omelet |
| **paisana** | paheessahnah | omelet with potatoes, peas, prawns |
| **de patatas** | day pahtahtahss | potato omelet |
| **de queso** | day kayssoa | cheese omelet |
| **al ron** | ahl ron | rum omelet |
| **de setas** | day saytahss | mushroom omelet |

EATING OUT

## Paella

An immensely popular dish along Spain's Mediterranean coast, *paella* actually refers to the large metal pan traditionally used for making rice dishes in the Valencia region. Basically, the *paella* dish is made of golden saffron rice garnished with meat, fish, seafood and/or vegetables. Here are four of the most popular ways of preparing *paella:*

| | |
|---|---|
| **catalana** (kahtah**lah**nah) | spicy pork sausages, pork, squid, tomato, chili pepper, peas; the same dish is sometimes referred to as *arroz a la catalana* |
| **marinera** (mahree**nay**rah) | fish and seafood only |
| **valenciana** (bahlayn**thyah**nah) | chicken, shrimp, mussels, prawns, squid, peas, tomato, chili pepper, garlic—it's the classic *paella* |
| **zamorana** (thamoa**rah**nah) | ham, pork loin, pig's trotters (feet), chili pepper |

Another rice dish is called *arroz a la cubana* (ahr**roth** ah lah koo**bhah**nah) made with white rice, fried eggs and bananas and a savoury tomato sauce.

## Fish and seafood

Don't miss the opportunity to sample some of the wide variety of fresh fish and seafood in coastal areas.

| | | |
|---|---|---|
| I'd like some fish. | **Quisiera pescado.** | kee**ssyay**rah pay**skahd**hoa |
| What kind of seafood do you have? | **¿Qué tipo de mariscos tiene usted?** | kay **tee**poa day mah**rees**koass **tyay**nay oos**taydh** |
| | | |
| almejas | ahl**mehk**hahss | clams |
| anchoas | ahn**choa**ahss | anchovies |
| anguilas | ahn**gee**lahss | eel |
| arenques | ah**rehn**kayss | herring |
| atún | ah**toon** | tunny (tuna) |
| bacalao | bahkah**lah**oa | cod |
| besugo | bay**ssoo**goa | (sea) bream |
| bonito | boa**nee**toa | tunny (tuna) |
| boquerones | boakayroa**nayss** | whitebait |

EATING OUT

| caballa | kahbhahlyah | mackerel |
| calamares | kahlahmahrayss | squid |
| cangrejo | kahngrehkhoa | crab |
| chipirones | cheepeeroanayss | baby squid |
| cigalas | theegahlahss | crayfish |
| congrio | koangryoa | conger eel |
| escarcho | ayskahrchoa | roach |
| lampresas | lahmprehssahss | lamprey |
| langosta | lahngoastah | spiny lobster |
| langostinos | lahngoasteenoass | crawfish |
| lenguado | layngwahdhoa | sole |
| merluza | mayrloothah | hake |
| mero | mehroa | seabass |
| moluscos | moalooskoass | mussels |
| mújol | mookhoal | mullet |
| ostras | ostrahss | oysters |
| perca | pehrkah | perch |
| percebes | pehrthaybhayss | goose barnacles |
| pescadilla | peskahdheelyah | whiting |
| pez espada | pehth ayspahdhah | swordfish |
| pulpitos | poolpeetoass | baby octopus |
| pulpo | poolpoa | octopus |
| quisquillas | keeskeelyahss | shrimp |
| rape | rahpay | monkfish |
| rodaballo | roadhahbhahlyoa | turbot |
| salmón | sahlmon | salmon |
| salmonetes | sahlmoanaytayss | red mullet |
| sardinas | sahrdeenahoo | sardines |
| pequeñas | paykayñahss | sprats |
| trucha | troochah | trout |
| venera | baynayrah | scallops |

You'll want to try the spicy fish and seafood stew called *zarzuela* (thahr**thway**lah)—the pride of Catalonia.

| baked | **al horno** | ahl oarnoa |
| cured | **en salazón** | ayn sahlahthon |
| deep fried | **a la romana** | ah lah roamahnah |
| fried | **frito** | freetoa |
| grilled | **a la parrilla** | ah lah pahrreelyah |
| marinated | **en escabeche** | ayn ayskahbhaychay |
| poached | **hervido** | ayrbeedhoa |
| sautéed | **salteado** | sahltehahdhoa |
| smoked | **ahumado** | ahoomahdhoa |
| steamed | **cocido al vapor** | koatheedhoa ahl bahpor |

## Meat

Though beef is neither as plentiful nor as tender as we're accustomed to at home, there's one cut of beef you'll enjoy—*solomillo* (soaloa**mee**lyoa)—roughly equivalent to a tenderloin steak. The delicate milk-fed veal is delicious. Kid goat and sucking pig generally feed on mountain rosemary and thyme which give a unique flavour to their flesh.

| I'd like some... | Quisiera... | keessyayrah |
|---|---|---|
| beef | **carne de buey** | **kahr**nay day bway |
| lamb | **carne de cordero** | **kahr**nay day koard**ay**roa |
| pork | **carne de cerdo** | **kahr**nay day **thehr**doa |
| veal | **carne de ternera** | **kahr**nay day tehr**nay**rah |
| **biftec** | beef**tayk** | beef steak |
| **cabrito** | kah**bree**toa | kid goat |
| **carne picada** | **kahr**nay pee**kah**dhah | minced meat |
| **carnero** | kahr**nay**roa | mutton |
| **chuletas** | choo**lay**tahss | chops |
| **corazón** | koarah**thon** | heart |
| **criadillas** | kreeah**dhee**lyahss | sweetbreads (glands) |
| **filete** | fee**lay**tay | fillet |
| **hígado** | **ee**gahdhoa | liver |
| **jamón** | khah**mon** | ham |
| **lechón** | lay**chon** | sucking pig |
| **morcilla** | moar**thee**lyah | black pudding (blood sausage) |
| **paletilla** | pahlay**tee**lyah | shank |
| **patas** | **pah**tahss | trotters (feet) |
| **pierna** | **pyehr**nah | leg |
| **rabo de buey** | **rah**bhoa day bway | oxtail |
| **riñones** | ree**ñoa**nayss | kidneys |
| **salchichas** | sahl**chee**chahss | sausages |
| **sesos** | **sayss**oass | brains |
| **solomillo de cerdo** | soaloa**mee**lyoa day **thehr**doa | terderloin steak of pork |
| **tocino** | toa**thee**noa | bacon |
| **toro de lidia** | **toa**roa day **lee**dyah | beef from the corrida |

| **callos a la madrileña** (**kahl**yoass ah lah mahdree**lay**ñah) | tripe in piquant sauce with spicy pork sausage and tomatoes |
|---|---|
| **empanada gallega** (aympah**nah**dhah gah**lyay**gah) | tenderloin of pork, onions and chilli peppers in a pie |

**pimientos a la riojana**
(peemyayntoass ah lah ryoakhahnah)
sweet peppers stuffed with minced meat

**riñones al jerez**
(reeñyoanayss ahl khehrayth)
kidneys braised in sherry

## Game and fowl

Chicken is prepared in scores of ways in Spain. In the north, rabbit is a favourite dish—sometimes even prepared with chocolate!

| I'd like some game. | Quisiera carne de caza. | keessyayrah kahrnay day kahthah |
|---|---|---|
| What poultry dishes do you have? | ¿Qué tipo de ave tiene usted? | kay teepoa day ahbhay tyaynay oostaydh |
| capón | kahpon | capon |
| codorniz | koädoarneeth | quail |
| conejo | koanaykhoa | rabbit |
| faisán | faheessahn | pheasant |
| ganso | gahnsoa | goose |
| higaditos de pollo | eegahdheetoass day poalyoa | chicken liver |
| liebre | lyehbray | hare |
| pato | pahtoa | duck/duckling |
| pavo | pahbhoa | turkey |
| perdíz | pehrdeeth | partridge |
| pichón | peechön | pidgeon |
| pollo | poalyoa | chicken |
| muslo de pollo | moosloa day poalyoa | chicken leg |
| pechuga de pollo | paychoogah day poalyoa | breast of chicken |
| pollo asado | poalyoa ahssahdhoa | roast chicken |
| pollo a la brasa | poalyoa ah lah brahssah | grilled chicken |
| venado | baynahdhoa | venison |

**conejo al ajillo**
(koanaykhoa ahl ahkheelyoa)
rabbit with garlic

**menestra de pollo**
(maynaystrah day poalyoa)
casserole of chicken and vegetables

**perdices estofadas**
(pehrdeethayss aystoafahdhahss)
partridges served in a white-wine sauce

EATING OUT

## How do you like your meat?

| | | |
|---|---|---|
| baked | **al horno** | ahl **oar**noa |
| braised | **estofado** | aystoa**fahd**hoa |
| braised in casserole | **en salsa** | ayn **sahl**ssah |
| fried | **frito** | **free**toa |
| grilled (broiled) | **a la parrilla** | ah lah pahr**reel**yah |
| pot roasted | **en su jugo** | an soo **khoo**goa |
| roast | **al horno** | ahl **oar**noa |
| sautéed | **salteado** | sahlteh**ahd**hoa |
| stewed | **estofado** | aystoa**fahd**hoa |
| | | |
| rare | **poco hecho** | **poa**koa **ay**choa |
| medium | **regular** | reh**goo**lahr |
| well-done | **muy hecho** | mwee **ay**choa |

### Sauces

Many meat, fish or vegetable dishes are dressed or braised in a light, delicate sauce. Here are the names of some well-known preparations:

**salsa allioli**
(**sahl**sah ah**lyoa**lee)
garlic sauce

**a la catalana**
(ah lah kahtah**lah**nah)
sauce of tomatoes and green peppers

**en escabeche**
(ayn ayskah**bhay**chay)
sweet and sour sauce

**salsa romesco**
(**sahl**sah roa**mays**koa)
green peppers, pimentos, garlic; popular chilled dressing for fish on the east cost around Tarragona

**a la Vasca**
(ah lah **bahs**kah)
parsley, peas, garlic; a delicate green dressing for fish in the Basque country

## Vegetables

Here's a savoury vegetable dish you're sure to like. It goes well with roast chicken or other roasted and grilled meats.

| | | |
|---|---|---|
| **pisto**<br>(peestoa) | | a stew of green peppers, onions, tomatoes and baby marrow (zucchini); in Catalonia it's called *samfaina,* and you might see it referred to as *frito de verduras.* |

| | | |
|---|---|---|
| **achicoria** | ahcheekoareeah | endive (US chicory) |
| **alcachofas** | ahlkahchoafahss | artichoke |
| **alcaparras** | ahlkahpahrrahss | capers |
| **apio** | ahpyoa | celery |
| **arroz** | ahrroth | rice |
| **berenjena** | bayraynkhaynah | aubergine (eggplant) |
| **calabacín** | kahlahbhatheen | baby marrow (zucchini) |
| **cebolla** | thayboalyah | onion |
| **champiñones** | chahmpeeñoanayss | mushrooms |
| **chirivías** | cheereebheeahss | parsnips |
| **chufa** | choofah | galingale |
| **coles de bruselas** | koalayss day broossaylahss | brussels sprouts |
| **coliflor** | koleeflor | cauliflower |
| **escarola** | ayskahroalah | chicory (US endive) |
| **espárragos** | ayspahrrahgoass | asparagus |
| **espinacas** | ayspeenahkahss | spinach |
| **garbanzos** | gahrbahnthoass | chick-peas |
| **guindilla** | geendeelyah | pimento |
| **guisantes** | geessahntayss | peas |
| **habas** | ahbhahss | broad beans |
| **judías blancas** | khoodheeahss blahnkahss | navy beans |
| **judías verdes** | khoodheeahss behrdayss | green beans |
| **lechuga** | laychoogah | lettuce |
| **lentejas** | layntaykhahss | lentils |
| **lombarda** | loambahrdah | red cabbage |
| **maíz** | maheeth | maize (corn) |
| **patatas** | pahtahtahss | potatoes |
| **pepinillos** | paypeeneelyoass | gherkins |
| **pepino** | paypeenoa | cucumber |
| **perejil** | payraykheel | parsley |
| **pimientos morrones** | peemyayntoass moarroanayss | sweet red peppers |
| **puerros** | pwayrroass | leeks |
| **rábanos** | rahbhahnoass | radishes |
| **remolacha** | raymoalahchah | beetroot |

| repollo | raypoalyoa | cabbage |
| tomates | toamahtayss | tomatoes |
| trufas | troofahss | truffles |
| zanahorias | thahnahoaryahss | carrots |

## Cheese

You'll seldom get a cheeseboard in Spanish restaurants. Some well-known Spanish cheeses are listed below. It'd be well to specify the cheese you'd like, otherwise you might be given imported cheese.

| burgos (boorgoass) | A favourite soft, creamy cheese named after the province from which it originates |
| cabrales (kahbrahlayss) | A tangy goat's milk cheese somewhat similar to blue cheese or roquefort; its flavour varies depending upon the mountain region in which is was produced. |
| mahón (mahon) | A goat's milk cheese of the Mahon Isle in the Baleares |
| manchego (mahnchaygoa) | Produced from ewe's milk, this hard cheese from La Mancha is particularly nourishing. The quality can vary but the best manchego is said to come from Ciudad Real. Its colour can vary from milky white to golden yellow. |
| perilla (pehreelyah) | A firm, bland cheese made from cow's milk; it's sometimes known as teta. Another cheese called San Simón resembles perilla both in flavour and texture. |
| roncal (ronkahl) | One of the most popular cheeses in northern Spain, it's hand-pressed, salted and smoked. This processing gives its rind a leathery appearance. Made from ewe's milk, roncal has a sharp taste. |
| villalón (beelyahlon) | Made from ewe's milk, it's curdled in two or three hours. Its curd is drained in bags, then pressed into moulds, salted and washed. |

EATING OUT

# Fruit

| Do you have fresh fruit? | ¿Tiene usted fruta fresca? | tyaynay oostaydh frootah frehskah |
| --- | --- | --- |
| I'd like a (fresh) fruit cocktail. | Quisiera una ensalada de fruta (fresca). | keessyayrah oonah aynsahlahdhah day frootah (frehskah) |

| albaricoques | ahlbahreekoakayss | apricots |
| --- | --- | --- |
| almendras | ahlmayndrahss | almonds |
| avellanas | ahbhaylyahnahss | hazelnuts |
| castañas | kahstahñahss | chestnuts |
| cerezas | thayraythahss | cherries |
| ciruelas | theerwaylahss | plums, prunes |
| coco | koakoa | coconut |
| dátiles | dahtoolayss | dates |
| frambuesas | frahmbwayssahss | raspberries |
| fresas | frayssahss | strawberries |
| granadas | grahnahdhahss | pomegranates |
| grosellas | groassaylyahss | red currants |
| higos | eegoass | figs |
| lima | leemah | lime |
| limón | leemon | lemon |
| mandarina | mahndahreenah | tangerine |
| manzana | mahnthahnah | apple |
| melocotón | mayloakoaton | peach |
| melón | maylon | melon |
| naranja | nahrahnkhah | orange |
| nueces | nwaythayss | walnuts |
| nueces variadas | nwaythayss bahryahdhahss | assorted nuts |
| pasas | pahssahss | raisins |
| pera | pehrah | pear |
| piña | peeñah | pineapple |
| plátano | plahtahnoa | banana |
| pomelo | poamayloa | grapefruit |
| ruibarbo | rweebhahrboa | rhubarb |
| sandía | sahndeeah | watermelon |
| uvas | oobhahss | grapes |

EATING OUT

## Dessert

If you've survived all the courses on the menu, you may want to say:

| | | |
|---|---|---|
| I'd like a dessert, please. | **Quisiera un postre por favor.** | keessyayrah oon poastray por fahbhor |
| Something light, please. | **Algo ligero, por favor.** | ahlgoa leekhayroa por fahbhor |
| Just a small portion. | **Una ración pequeña.** | oonah rahthyon paykayñah |

If you aren't sure what to order, ask the waiter:

| | | |
|---|---|---|
| What do you have for dessert? | **¿Qué tiene de postre?** | kay tyaynay day poastray |
| What do you recommend? | **¿Qué me aconseja?** | kay may ahkoansehkhah |

| | | |
|---|---|---|
| arroz con leche | ahrroth kon laychay | rice pudding |
| bizcocho | beethkoachoa | sponge cake |
| crema catalana | kraymah kahtahlahnah | caramel pudding |
| flan | flahn | caramel pudding |
| fritos | freetoass | fritters |
| galletas | gahlyaytahss | biscuits (cookies) |
| helado | aylahdhoa | ice-cream |
| de chocolate | day choakoalahtay | chocolate |
| de fresa | day frayssah | strawberry |
| de vainilla | day bayneelyah | vanilla |
| mantecado | mahntehkahdhoa | enriched ice-cream |
| mazapán | mahthahpahn | marzipan |
| melocotón en almíbar | mayloakoaton ayn ahlmeebhahr | peaches in syrup |
| membrillo | maymbreelyoa | quince jelly cake |
| merengue | mayraynggay | meringue |
| pastas | pahstahss | biscuits (cookies) |
| pastel | pahstayl | cake |
| pastel de queso | pahstayl day kehssoa | cheesecake |
| tarta de almendras | tahrtah day ahlmayndrahss | almond tart |
| tarta de manzana | tahrtah day mahnthahnah | apple tart |
| tarta de moka | tahrtah day moakah | coffee-flavoured cake |
| tarta helada | tahrtah aylahdhah | ice-cream cake |
| tarteletas | tahrtaylaytahss | small tarts |
| turrón | toorron | nougat |
| tortitas | torteetahss | waffles |

## The bill

| | | |
|---|---|---|
| I'd like to pay. | **Quisiera pagar.** | keessyayrah pahgahr |
| We'd like to pay separately. | **Quisiéramos pagar separadamente.** | keessyayrahmoass pahgahr saypahrahdhahmayntay |
| You made a mistake in this bill, I think. | **Me parece que se ha equivocado usted en esta cuenta.** | may pahraythay kay say ah aykeebhoakahdhoa oostaydh ayn aystah kwayntah |
| What's this amount for? | **¿Para qué es esta cantidad?** | pahrah kay ayss aystah kahnteedhahdh |
| Is service included? | **¿Está el servicio incluido?** | aystah ayl sehrbeethyoa eenklooeedhoa |
| Is the cover charge included? | **¿Está el cubierto incluido?** | aystah ayl koobyehrtoa eenklooeedhoa |
| Is everything included? | **¿Está todo incluido?** | aystah toadhoa eenklooeedhoa |
| Do you accept traveller's cheques? | **¿Acepta usted cheques de viajero?** | ahthehptah oostaydh chaykayss day byahkhayroa |
| Thank you, this is for you. | **Gracias, esto es para usted.** | grahthyahss aystoa ayss pahrah oostaydh |
| That was a very good meal. | **Ha sido una comida excelente.** | ah seedhoa oonah koameedhah ayksaylayntay |
| We enjoyed it, thank you. | **Nos ha gustado, gracias.** | noss ah goostahdhoa grahthyahss |

> **SERVICIO INCLUIDO**
> SERVICE INCLUDED

**EATING OUT**

## Complaints

But perhaps you'll have something to complain about:

| | | |
|---|---|---|
| That's not what I ordered. I asked for... | **Esto no es lo que he pedido. He pedido...** | aystoa noa ayss loa kay ay pehdheedhoa. ay pehdheedhoa |
| May I change this? | **¿Puede cambiarme eso?** | pwaydhay kahmbyahrmay ayssoa |

| The meat is... | Esta carne está... | aystah kahrnay aystah |
| overdone | demasiado hecha | daymahssyahdhoa ehchah |
| underdone | poco hecha | poakoa ehchah |
| too rare | demasiado cruda | daymahssyahdhoa kroodhah |
| too tough | demasiado dura | daymahssyahdhoa doora |
| This is too... | Esto está... | aystoa aystah |
| bitter/salty/sweet | amargo/salado/dulce | ahmahrgoa/sahlahdhoa/doolthay |
| The food is cold. | La comida está fría. | lah koameedhah aystah freeah |
| This isn't fresh. | Esto no está fresco. | aystoa noa aystah frayskoa |
| What's taking you so long? | ¿Por qué se demora tanto? | por kay say daymoarah tahntoa |
| Where are our drinks? | ¿Dónde están nuestras bebidas? | doanday aystahn nways-trahss behbheedhahss |
| This isn't clean. | Esto no está limpio. | aystoa noa aystah leempyoa |
| Would you ask the head waiter to come over? | ¿Quiere usted decirle al jefe que venga? | keeayray oostaydh daytheerlay ahl khehfay kay bayngah |

## Drinks

### Aperitifs

For most Spaniards, a before-dinner *vermut* (behr**moot**—vermouth) or *jerez* (kheh**rayss**—sherry) is just as important as our cocktail or highball. Vermouth is rarely drunk neat (straight) but usually on the rocks or with seltzer water. Two of the favourite aperitif sherries are *amontillado* (ahmontee-**lyah**dhoa) or *manzanilla* (mahntha**neel**yah). Some Spaniards, on the other hand, content themselves with a glass of the local wine. You'll likely be given a dish of olives or nuts to nibble on with your sherry or vermouth. Or in a bar specializing in *tapas*, you can order other little delicacies.

## Wine

Though Spain is one of the world's principal producers of wine, the nation's *vino* —with the exception of sherry—is among the most unpredictable in terms of quality. Using outmoded techniques in both cultivating grapes and fermenting wine, the wine of a specific vineyard can vary considerably from one year to the next.

Some restaurants list their wine in a corner of the menu while others have them posted on a wall. As much of the country's wine doesn't travel well, don't expect an *hostería* to offer more than a few types of wine. Most of the wine must be drunk young so don't look too hard for vintage labels.

A government board permits some vintners to include *denominación de origen* on a bottle as an indication of the wine's quality. However, this designation is unreliable.

Uncontestably, Spain's best wine comes from Rioja, a region of Old Castile of which Logroño is the centre. Winemakers there add *garantía de origen* to wine they feel is of above average quality, and this term is a respected one. But other regions—notably Andalusia, Aragon, Catalonia, Navarre, New Castile, Toledo and Valdepeñas—produce quality wine, too. This is your opportunity to sample local wine, some of which is surprisingly good.

The general rule of thumb is that white wine goes well with fish and light meats while red wine is reserved for dark meats. A good rosé goes with almost anything. The chart on the following page will help you to choose your wine if you want to do some serious wine-tasting.

If you need help in choosing a wine, don't hesitate to ask the waiter. He'll often suggest a bottle of local renown, perhaps from the *patrón*'s own wine cellar.

EATING OUT

EATING OUT

| Type of wine | Examples | Accompanies |
|---|---|---|
| **sweet white wine** | A *moscatel* | desserts, custards, cakes, rice puddings, biscuits (cookies) |
| **light, dry white wine** | Much local white wine falls into this category; much of the white wine of Rioja, like *Monopole* | fish, seafood, *tapas*, cold meat, boiled meat, egg dishes like tortillas |
| **rosé** | López de Heredia, Marqués de Murrieta | goes with almost anything but especially cold dishes, eggs, pork, lamb, *paella* |
| **light-bodied red wine** | Many local wines come into this group; much of the Rioja red wine classifies, including *Viña Pomal* or the Catalonian *Priorato Reserva especial* | roast chicken, turkey, veal, lamb, beef fillet, ham, liver, quail, pheasant, stews, steaks, *zarzuela, paella, tortillas* |
| **full-bodied red wine** | sometimes a red wine of Tarragone, Alicante or Rioja can be classed in this category | duck, goose, kidneys, most game, tangy cheese like *cabrales*—in short, any strong-flavoured preparations |
| **sparkling wine** | *Xampañ* or *Cordoniu* | goes well with desserts and custards; if it's really dry you might try some as an aperitif or with shellfish, nuts, dried fruit |

| I'd like ... of ... | Quisiera ... de ... | keessyayrah...day |
|---|---|---|
| a carafe | una garrafa | oonah gahrrahfah |
| a bottle | una botella | oonah boataylyah |
| half bottle | media botella | maydhyah boataylyah |
| a glass | un vaso | oon bahssoa |
| a small glass | un chato | oon chahtoa |
| a litre | un litro | oon leetroa |
| I want a bottle of white/red wine. | Quiero una botella de vino blanco/ vino tinto. | kyayroa oonah boataylyah day beenoa blahnkoa/ beenoa teentoa |

If you enjoyed the wine, you may want to say:

| Please bring me another... | Tráigame otro/otra ... por favor. | trighgahmay oatroa/oatrah ...por fahbhor |
| Where does this wine come from? | ¿De dónde viene este vino? | day doanday byaynay aystay beenoa |

| red | tinto | teentoa |
|---|---|---|
| white | blanco | blahnkoa |
| rosé | rosé | rosé |
| | | |
| dry | seco | saykoa |
| full-bodied | de cuerpo | day kwehrpoa |
| light | liviano | leebyahnoa |
| sparkling | espumoso | ayspoomoassoa |
| sweet | dulce | doolthay |
| very dry | muy seco | mwee saykoa |

## Other alcoholic drinks

Cafés and bars in major cities and tourist centres usually have a good stock of foreign and domestic beer, wine and liquor—even some of your favourite brands. Off the beaten tourist track, however, brands will be largely local. Don't bother asking for any fancy cocktail or highball except in swank places or where signs are displayed saying *American bar*. Though not especially noted for its beer brewing you may want to sample local ale like *El Aguila especial* or *San Miguel especial*.

| | | |
|---|---|---|
| aniseed liqueur | **anís** | ahneess |
| aperitif | **aperitivo** | ahpayreeteebhoa |
| beer | **cerveza** | thehrbaythah |
| Bourbon | **Borbón** | boarbon |
| brandy | **coñac** | koañahk |
| cider | **sidra** | seedrah |
| cognac | **coñac** | koañahk |
| cordial | **licor** | leekor |
| gin | **ginebra** | kheenaybrah |
| gin-fizz | **ginebra con limón** | kheenaybrah kon leemon |
| gin and tonic | **ginebra con tónica** | kheenaybrah kon toaneekah |
| liqueur | **licor** | leekor |
| port | **vino de Oporto** | beenoa day oaportoa |
| rum | **ron** | ron |
| rum coke | **Cuba libre** | koobhah leebray |
| Scotch | **whisky escocés** | weeskee ayskoathayss |
| sherry | **jerez** | khehrayss |
| vermouth | **vermut** | behrmoot |
| vodka | **vodka** | bodkah |
| whisky | **whisky** | weeskee |
| whisky and soda | **whisky con soda** | weeskee kon sodhah |

| | | |
|---|---|---|
| glass | **un vaso** | oon bahssoa |
| bottle | **una botella** | oonah boataylyah |
| double (a double shot) | **doble** | doablay |
| neat (straight) | **solo** | soaloa |
| on the rocks | **con hielo** | kon yayloa |

If you'd like to sip a brandy after dinner, try a Spanish *coñac* like *Fundador* (foondah**dhor**) or *Carlos III* (**kahr**loass trayss). The Spaniards are also noted for their delicious liqueurs such as *Licor 43, Calisay,* or *Aromas de Montserrat.*

| | | |
|---|---|---|
| I'd like to try a glass of ..., please. | **Quisiera un vaso de ..., por favor.** | keessyayrah oon bahssoa day...por fahbhor |
| Are there any local specialities? | **¿Tiene alguna especialidad local?** | tyaynay ahlgoonah ayspaythyahleedhadh loakahl |
| Please bring me a ... of ... | **Tráigame un/una... de..., por favor.** | trighgahmay oon/oonah... day...por fahbhor |

Without question, the country's most renowned drink is its sherry. Like marsala, madeira and port wine, sherry has a bit of alcohol or brandy added to it—to "fortify" it—during its fermentation process.

Sherry was the first fortified wine to become popular in England and was used as a bracer to the damp weather of Britain. Back in Shakespeare's day it was called *sack* or *sherris sack*. *Sack* was derived from the Spanish *sacar* (to export) while the English wrote *Sherris* for the name of the town, *Jerez*, where sherry wine originated. Sherry can be divided into two groups:

| | |
|---|---|
| **fino**<br>(faanoa) | These are the pale, rich and dry sherries which make good aperitifs. The Spaniards themselves are especially fond of *amontillado* and *manzanilla*. Some of the best *finos* are *Tio Pepe* and *La Ina*. |
| **oloroso**<br>(oloarossoa) | These are the heavier, darker sherries which are sweetened before being bottled. They're fine after-dinner drinks. One exception is *amorosa* which is medium dry. Brown and cream sherries are full-bodied and slightly less fragrant than *finos*. |

> **¡SALUD!**
> (sahloodh)
> CHEERS!

**EATING OUT**

## Other beverages

| I'd like a/an... | Quisiera... | keessyayrah |
|---|---|---|
| (hot) chocolate | un chocolate (caliente) | oon choakoalahtay (kahlyayntay) |
| coffee | un café | oon kahfay |
| cup of coffee | una taza de café | oonah tahthah day kahfay |
| black coffee | café solo | kahfay soaloa |
| white coffee | un cortado | oon koartahdhoa |
| coffee with cream | café con crema | kahfay kon kraymah |
| espresso coffee | café exprés | kahfay ayksprayss |
| strong coffee | un corto | oon koartoa |

| fruit juice | un jugo de fruta | oon khoogoa day frootah |
| apple/grapefruit | manzana/pomelo | mahnthahnah/poamenloa |
| lemon/orange | limón/naranja | leemon/nahrahnkhah |
| pineapple/tomato | piña/tomate | peeñah/toamahtay |
| lemonade | una limonada | oonah leemoanahdhah |
| milk | leche | laychay |
| milkshake | un batido | oon bahteedhoa |
| mineral water | agua mineral | ahgwah meenayrahl |
| orangeade | una naranjada | oonah nahrahnkhahdhah |
| soda water | una soda | oonah soadhah |
| squash (fruit drink) | un batido | oon bahteedhoa |
| tea | un té | oon tay |
| with milk/lemon | con leche/con limón | kon laychay/kon leemon |
| iced tea | un té helado | oon tay aylahdhoa |
| tonic water | una tónica | oonah toaneekah |

## Eating light—Snacks

| I'll have one of those, please. | Déme uno de esos, por favor. | daymay oonoa day ayssoass por fahbhor |
| Give me two of these and one of those. | Déme dos de estos y uno de esos, por favor. | daymay doss day aystoass ee oonoa day ayssoass por fahbhor |
| to the left/to the right | a la izquierda/a la derecha | ah lah eethkyayrdah/ah lah dayraychah |
| above/below | encima/debajo | ayntheemah/daybhahkhoa |
| Please give me a / an / some... | Déme ... por favor. | daymay ... por fahbhor |
| biscuits (Br.) | galletas | gahlyaytahss |
| bread | pan | pahn |
| butter | mantequilla | mahntaykeelyah |
| cake | un pastel | oon pahstehl |
| candy | unos caramelos | oonoass kahrahmayloass |
| chocolate bar | una chocolatina | oonah choakoalahteenah |
| cookies | galletas | gahlyaytahss |
| ice-cream | un helado | oon aylahdhoa |
| pastry | pasteles | pahstaylayss |
| rolls | panecillos | pahnaytheelyoass |
| salad | una ensalada | oonah aynsahlahdhah |
| sweets | unos caramelos | oonoass kahrahmayloass |
| toast | unas tostadas | oonahss toastahdhahss |
| How much is that? | ¿Cuánto es? | kwahntoa ayss |

# Travelling around

**Plane**

Very brief—because at any airport or airline office you're sure to find someone who speaks English. But here are a few useful expressions you may want to know:

| | | |
|---|---|---|
| Is there a flight to Madrid? | ¿Hay algún vuelo a Madrid? | igh ahlgoon bwayloa ah mahdreedh |
| Is it a nonstop flight? | ¿Es un vuelo sin escalas? | ayss oon bwayloa seen ayskahlahss |
| When's the next plane to Barcelona? | ¿Cuándo sale el próximo avión para Barcelona? | kwahndoa sahlay ayl prokseemoa ahbhyon pahrah bahrthayloanah |
| Do I have to change planes? | ¿Tengo que hacer transbordo? | tayngoa kay ahthayr trahnsbordoa |
| Can I make a connection to Alicante? | ¿Puedo hacer conexión con un vuelo a Alicante? | pwaydhoa ahthayr koanayksyon kon oon bwayloa ah ahleekahntay |
| I'd like a ticket to London. | Quisiera un billete para Londres. | keessyayrah oon beelyay-tay pahrah loandrayss |
| What's the fare to Paris? | ¿Cuál es la tarifa a Paris? | kwahl ayss lah tahreefah ah pahreess |
| single (one-way) | ida | eedhah |
| return (roundtrip) | ida y vuelta | eedhah ee bwehltah |
| What time does the plane take off? | ¿A qué hora despega el avión? | ah kay oarah dayspaygah ayl ahbhyon |
| What time do I have to check in? | ¿A qué hora debo hacer la facturación? | ah kay oarah daybhoa ahthayr lah fahktoorah-thyon |
| What's the flight number? | ¿Cuál es el número del vuelo? | kwahl ayss ayl noomayroa day bwayloa |
| At what time do we arrive? | ¿A qué hora llegaremos? | ah kay oarah lyaygahraymoass |

| LLEGADA | SALIDA |
|---|---|
| ARRIVAL | DEPARTURE |

### Train

If you're worried about railway tickets or time-tables, go to a travel agency where they speak English or see the desk-clerk at your hotel.

Keep in mind that Spaniards don't attach the same importance to punctuality that we do. Trains may run on time, and then again they may not. First-class coaches are comfortable; second-class, adequate.

### Types of trains

| | |
|---|---|
| **TALGO, TER** (tahlgoa, tehr) | Luxury diesel express, air-conditioned, first and second class; supplementary fare required |
| **TAF** (tahf) | Diesel express, not used on the main lines |
| **Expreso** (ayssprayssoa) | Long-distance night train, stopping at main stations |
| **Rápido** (rahpeedhoa) | Express, stopping at main stations |
| **Automotor** (owtoamoator) | Used for short distances, similar to the *omnibus* |
| **Omnibus** (omneebhooss) | Local train stopping at all stations |

### Long-distance bus

Travel by bus is good if you want to visit out-of-the-way places. There's no cross-country bus line. Most buses only serve towns and villages within a region or province, or they link the provincial capital with Madrid if there's no rail service.

*Note:* Most of the phrases on the following pages can be used or adapted for bus travel.

## To the railway station

| | | |
|---|---|---|
| Where's the railway station ? | ¿Dónde está la estación de ferrocarril ? | doanday aystah lah aystahthyon day fehrrokahrreel |
| Taxi, please ! | ¡Taxi ! por favor. | tahksee por fahbhor |
| Take me to the railway station. | Lléveme a la estación de ferrocarril. | lyaybhaymay ah lah aystahthyon day fehrrokahrreel |
| What's the fare ? | ¿Cuál es la tarifa ? | kwahl ayss lah tahreefah |

---

| | |
|---|---|
| **INFORMACION TURISTICA** | TOURIST INFORMATION |
| **CAMBIO DE MONEDA** | CURRENCY EXCHANGE |

---

## Where's the ... ?

| | | |
|---|---|---|
| Where is / are the ... ? | ¿Dónde está / están ... ? | doanday aystah / aystahn |
| booking office | la oficina de reservas | lah oafeetheenah day rayssayrbahss |
| buffet | el buffet | ayl boofay |
| currency-exchange office | la oficina de cambio de moneda | lah oafeetheenah day kahmbyoa day moanaydnah |
| information office | la oficina de información | lah oafeetheenah day eenformahthyon |
| left-luggage office (baggage check) | la consigna | lah konseegnah |
| lost-property (lost-and-found) office | la oficina de objetos perdidos | lah oafeetheenah day obkhaytoass pehrdeedhoass |
| luggage lockers | los casilleros con llave para el equipaje | loss kahsseelyayroass kon lyahbhay pahrah ayl aykeepahkhay |
| news-stand | el puesto de periódicos | ayl pwaystoa day payryodheekoass |
| platform 7 | el andén 7 | ayl ahndayn 7 |
| restaurant | el restaurante | ayl raystowrahntay |
| ticket office | la taquilla | lah tahkeelyah |
| toilets | los servicios | loss sehrbeethyoass |
| waiting room | la sala de espera | lah sahlah day ayspayrah |

FOR TAXI, see page 27

## Inquiries

| When is the...train to Granada? | ¿A qué hora sale el ...tren para Granada? | ah kay oarah sahlay ayl... trayn pahrah grahnahdhah |
| first / last / next | primer / último / próximo | preemayr / oolteemoa / prokseemoa |
| What time does the train for Valencia leave? | ¿A qué hora sale el tren para Valencia? | ah kay oarah sahlay ayl trayn pahrah bahlaynthyah |
| What's the fare to Malaga? | ¿Cuál es la tarifa para Málaga? | kwahl ayss lah tahreefah pahrah mahlahgah |
| Is it a through train? | ¿Es un tren directo? | ayss oon trayn deerehktoa |
| Will the train leave on time? | ¿Saldrá el tren a su hora? | sahldrah ayl trayn ah soo oarah |
| What time does the train arrive at Santander? | ¿A qué hora llega el tren a Santander? | ah kay oarah lyaygah ayl trayn ah sahntahndayr |
| Is there a dining-car on the train? | ¿Hay coche restaurante en el tren? | igh koachay raystowrahntay ayn ayl trayn |
| Is there a sleeping-car on the train? | ¿Hay coche cama en el tren? | igh koachay kahmah ayn ayl trayn |
| Does the train stop at Gerona? | ¿Para el tren en Gerona? | pahrah ayl trayn ayn khayroanah |
| What platform does the train for Barcelona leave from? | ¿De qué andén sale el tren para Barcelona? | day kay ahndayn sahlay ayl trayn pahrah bahrthayloanah |
| What platform does the train from... arrive at? | ¿A qué andén llega el tren de...? | ah kay ahndayn lyaygah ayl trayn day |
| I'd like to buy a timetable. | Quisiera comprar una guía de ferrocarriles. | keessyayrah komprahr oonah geeah day fehrrokahrreelayss |

| ENTRADA | ENTRANCE |
| SALIDA | EXIT |
| A LOS ANDENES | TO THE PLATFORMS |

| | |
|---|---|
| Es un tren directo. | It's a through train. |
| Usted tiene que hacer transbordo en... | You have to change at... |
| Transborde en... y tome un tren de cercanías. | Change at... and get a local train. |
| El andén... está... | Platform... is... |
| allí / arriba / a la izquierda / a la derecha | over there / upstairs / on the left / on the right |
| Hay un tren para Barcelona a las... | There's a train to Barcelona at... |
| Su tren sale del andén... | Your train will leave from platform... |
| Habrá una demora de ... minutos. | There'll be a delay of ... minutes. |

## Tickets

| | | |
|---|---|---|
| I want a ticket to Bilbao. | Quiero un billete para Bilbao. | kyayroa oon beelyaylay pahrah beelbahoa |
| single (one-way) | ida | eedhah |
| return (roundtrip) | ida y vuelta | eedhah ee bwehltah |
| first class | primera clase | preemayrah klahssay |
| second class | segunda clase | saygoondah klahssay |
| Isn't it half price for the boy / girl? | ¿No paga medio billete el niño / la niña? | noa pahgah maydhyoa beelyaytay ayl neeñoa / lah neeñah |
| He's / She's 13. | El / Ella tiene 13 años. | ayl / aylyah tyaynay 13 ahñoass |

| | |
|---|---|
| ¿Primera o segunda clase? | First or second class? |
| ¿Ida o ida y vuelta? | Single or return (one-way or roundtrip)? |
| ¿Cuántos años tiene él / ella? | How old is he / she? |

TRAVELLING AROUND

## All aboard...

| | | |
|---|---|---|
| Is this the right platform for the train to Paris? | ¿Es éste el andén del tren para París? | ayss aystay ayl ahnday dayl trayn pahrah pahreess |
| Is this the train to Madrid? | ¿Es éste el tren para Madrid? | ayss aystay ayl trayn pahrah mahdreedh |
| Excuse me. May I get by? | Perdóneme. ¿Puedo pasar? | pehrdoanaymay. pwaydhoa pahssahr |
| Is this seat taken? | ¿Está ocupado éste asiento? | aystah oakoopahdhoa aystay ahssyayntoa |

**PROHIBIDO FUMAR**
NO SMOKING

| | | |
|---|---|---|
| I think that's my seat. | Creo que ese es mi asiento. | krayoa kay ayssay ayss mee ahssyayntoa |
| Would you let me know before we get to Valencia? | ¿Me avisaría antes de llegar a Valencia? | may ahbheessahreeah ahntayss day lyaygahr ah bahlaynthyah |
| What station is this? | ¿Qué estación es esta? | kay aystahthyon ayss aystah |
| How long does the train stop here? | ¿Cuánto tiempo para el tren aquí? | kwahntoa tyaympoa pahrah ayl trayn ahkee |
| When do we get to Barcelona? | ¿Cuándo llegamos a Barcelona? | kwahndoa lyaygahmoass ah bahrthayloanah |

Sometime on the journey the ticket-collector *(el revisor)* will come around and say: "*Sus billetes, por favor!*" (tickets, please!)

### Eating

If you want a full meal in the dining-car, you may have to get a ticket from the steward who'll come round to your compartment. There are usually two sittings for breakfast, lunch and dinner. State which one you prefer:

| | | |
|---|---|---|
| First / Second sitting, please. | Primer / Segundo turno, por favor. | preemayr / saygoondoa toornoa por fahbhor |

You can get snacks and drinks in the buffet-car and in the dining-car when it isn't being used for meals. At the larger stations an attendant with a refreshment cart walks alongside the train and takes orders through the window.

| Where's the dining-car? | ¿Dónde está el coche comedor? | doanday aystah ayl koachay koamaydhor |

## Sleeping

| Are there any free compartments in the sleeping-car? | ¿Hay un departamento libre en el coche cama? | igh oon daypahrtah-mayntoa leebray ayn ayl koachay kahmah |
| Where's the sleeping-car? | ¿Dónde está el coche cama? | doanday aystah ayl koachay kahmah |
| Where's my berth? | ¿Dónde está mi litera? | doanday aystah mee leetayrah |
| Compartments 18 and 19, please. | Departamentos 18 y 19, por favor. | daypahrtahmayntoass 18 ee 19 por fahbhor |
| I'd like a lower berth. | Quisiera una litera en la parte inferior. | keessyayrah oonah leetayrah ayn lah pahrtay eenfayryor |
| Would you make up our berths? | ¿Nos podrá hacer usted la cama? | noss poadrah ahthayr oostaydh lah kahmah |
| Would you call me at 7 o'clock? | ¿Me podrá llamar usted a las 7? | may poadrah lyahmahr oostaydh ah lahss 7 |
| Would you bring me some coffee in the morning? | ¿Me podrá traer usted café por la mañana? | may poadrah trahehr oostaydh kahfay por lah mahñahnah |

## Baggage and porters

| Porter! | ¡Mozo! | moathoa |
| Can you help me with my bags? | ¿Puede usted ayudarme con mi equipaje? | pwaydhay oostaydh ahyoodhahrmay kon mee aykeepahkhay |
| Please put them down here. | Por favor, póngalas aquí. | por fahbhor poangahlahss ahkee |
| Can I register these bags? | ¿Puedo facturar estas maletas? | pwaydhoa fahktoorahr aystahss mahlaytahss |

FOR PORTERS, also see page 24

TRAVELLING AROUND

## Lost!

We hope you'll have no need for the following phrases on your trip ... but just in case:

| | | |
|---|---|---|
| Where's the lost-property (lost-and-found) office? | ¿Dónde está la oficina de objetos perdidos? | doanday aystah lah oafeetheenah day obkhaytoass pehrdeedhoass |
| I've lost my... | He perdido mi... | ay pehrdeedhoa mee |
| this morning | esta mañana | aystah mahñahnah |
| yesterday | ayer | ahyehr |
| I lost it in... | Lo perdí en... | loa pehrdee ayn |
| It's very valuable. | Tiene mucho valor. | tyaynay moochoa bahlor |

## Underground (subway)

The *Metro* in Madrid and Barcelona corresponds to the London underground or to the subway in America.

The fare is the same irrespective of the distance. If you use the *Metro* regularly, get a book of tickets (*un taco*—oon **tah**koa). This'll mean a small saving on fares.

The underground is open from 6 to 1 a.m. Certain seats in the compartments are reserved for the physically handicapped.

| | | |
|---|---|---|
| Where's the nearest underground station? | ¿Dónde está la estación de Metro más cercana? | doanday aystah lah aystahthyon day maytroa mahss thehrkahnah |
| Does this train go to...? | ¿Vá este tren a...? | bah aystay trayn ah |
| Where do I change for...? | ¿Dónde tengo que hacer transbordo para...? | doanday tayngoa kay ahthayr trahnsbordoa pahrah |
| Is the next station...? | ¿Es...la próxima estación? | ayss...lah prokseemah aystahthyon |

## Bus

In most buses, you pay as you enter. In some rural buses, you may find the driver also acting as the conductor.

In major cities it may be worthwhile to get a runabout ticket or a booklet of tickets.

If a bus carries the sign *completo,* it means that it's full.

| | | |
|---|---|---|
| I'd like a booklet of tickets. | **Quisiera un taco de billetes.** | keessyayrah oon tahkoa day beelyaytayss |
| Where can I get a bus to the beach? | **¿Dónde puedo tomar un autobús para la playa?** | doanday pwaydhoa toamahr oon owtoabhooss pahrah lah plahyah |
| What bus do I take for the university? | **¿Qué autobús debo tomar para la Universidad?** | kay owtoabhooss daybhoa toamahr pahrah lah ooneebhohrseedhahdh |
| Where's the...? | **¿Dónde está...?** | doanday aystah |
| bus stop | **la parada de autobuses** | lah pahrahdha day owtoabhoossayss |
| terminus | **la terminal** | lah tehrmeenahl |
| When is the...bus to the Prado? | **¿A qué hora es el. autobús para El Prado?** | ah kay oarah ayss ayl... owtoabhooss pahrah ayl prahdhoa |
| first / last / next | **primer / último / próximo** | preemayr / oolteemoa / prokseemoa |
| How often do the buses to the town centre run? | **¿Cada cuánto pasan los autobuses para el centro?** | kahdhah kwahntoa pahssahn loss owtoabhoossayss pahrah ayl thayntroa |
| How much is the fare to...? | **¿Cuánto es la tarifa para...?** | kwahntoa ayss lah tahreefah pahrah |
| Do I have to change buses? | **¿Tengo que hacer transbordo?** | tayngoa kay ahthayr trahnsbordoa |
| How long does the journey take? | **¿Cuánto dura el viaje?** | kwahntoa doorah ayl byahkhay |
| Will you tell me when to get off? | **¿Me diría usted cuándo tengo que apearme?** | may deereeah oostaydh kwahndoa tayngoa kay ahpayahrmay |
| I want to get off at the cathedral. | **Quiero apearme en la Catedral.** | kyayroa ahpayahrmay ayn lah kahtaydrahl |

| Please let me off at the next stop. | **Por favor, pare en la próxima parada.** | por fah**bhor** pah**ray** ayn lah **proks**eemah pah**rahd**dah |
| May I please have my luggage? | **¿Me podría dar mi equipaje, por favor?** | may poa**dree**ah dahr mee aykeepah**khay** por fah**bhor** |

---

| **PARADA DE AUTOBUS** | REGULAR BUS STOP |
| **SOLO PARA A PETICION** | STOPS ON REQUEST |

---

## Boat service

If you have the time, a trip by sea is a relaxing way to travel from the Spanish mainland to the Balearic and Canary islands. There's daily boat service from the mainland to the Baleares—often an overnight trip. Maritime service to the Canaries is far less frequent; the voyage takes 36–48 hours. There are different classes of travel but fares are moderate—even if you're travelling with your car on a ferry.

The phrases under the entry "Trains" can also come in useful during a boat-trip.

## Other means of transport

| bicycle | **la bicicleta** | lah beethee**klay**tah |
| boat | **el barco** | ayl **bahr**koa |
| motorboat | **el barco de motor** | ayl **bahr**koa day moa**tor** |
| rowing-boat | **el barco de remos** | ayl **bahr**koa day **reh**moass |
| sailing-boat | **el barco de vela** | ayl **bahr**koa day **bay**lah |
| helicopter | **el helicóptero** | ayl aylee**kop**tayroa |
| hitch-hiking | **el auto-stop** | ayl **ow**toa-**stop** |
| horseback riding | **montar a caballo** | moan**tahr** ah kah**bhah**lyoa |
| hovercraft | **el aerodeslizador** | ayl ahayroadhaysleethah-**dhor** |
| motorcycle | **la motocicleta** | lah moatoathee**klay**tah |

# Around and about—Sightseeing

Here we're more concerned with the cultural aspect of life than with entertainment; and, for the moment, with towns rather than the countryside. If you want a guide book, ask...

| | | |
|---|---|---|
| Can you recommend a good guide book for...? | ¿Puede usted recomendarme una buena guía de...? | pwaydhay oostaydh rehkoamayndahrmay oonah bwaynah geeah day |
| Is there a tourist office? | ¿Hay una oficina de turismo? | igh oonah oafeetheenah day tooreesmoa |
| Where's the tourist office/information centre? | ¿Dónde está la oficina de turismo/información? | doanday aystah lah oafeetheenah day tooreesmoa/eenformahthyon |
| What are the main points of interest? | ¿Cuáles son los principales puntos de interés? | kwahlayss son loss preentheepahlayss poontoass day eentayrayss |
| We're here for... | Estamos aquí... | aystahmoass ahkee |
| only a few hours | sólo unas pocas horas | soaloa oonahss pokahss oarahss |
| a day | un día | oon deeah |
| three days | tres días | trayss deeahss |
| a week | una semana | oonah saymahnah |
| Can you recommend a sightseeing tour? | ¿Puede usted recomendarme un recorrido turístico? | pwaydhay oostaydh rehkoamayndahrmay oon raykorreedhoa tooreesteekoa |
| Where does the bus start from? | ¿De dónde sale el autobús? | day doanday sahlay ayl owtoabhooss |
| Will it pick us up at the hotel? | ¿Nos recogerá en el hotel? | noss rehkoakhayrah ayn ayl oatehl |
| What bus do we take? | ¿Qué autobús necesitamos? | kay owtoabhooss naythaysseetahmoass |
| How much does the tour cost? | ¿Cuánto cuesta el recorrido? | kwahntoa kwaystah ayl rehkorreedhoa |
| What time does the tour start? | ¿A qué hora empieza el recorrido? | ah kay oarah aympyaythah ayl rehkorreedhoa |
| We'd like to rent a car for the day. | Nos gustaría alquilar un coche para todo el día. | noss goostahreeah ahlkeelahr oon koachay pahrah toadhoa ayl deeah |

FOR TIME OF THE DAY, see page 178

SIGHTSEEING

| Is there an English-speaking guide? | ¿Hay algún guía que hable inglés? | igh ahlgoon geeah kay ahblay eenglayss |
| Where is/are the...? | ¿Dónde está/están...? | doanday aystah/aystahn |
| abbey | la abadía | lah ahbhadheeah |
| aquarium | el acuarium | ayl ahkwahryoom |
| art gallery | la galería de arte | lah gahlayreeah day ahrtay |
| artist's quarter | el barrio de los artistas | ayl bahrreeoa day loss ahrteestahss |
| botanical gardens | el jardín botánico | ayl khahrdeen boatahneekoa |
| business district | el barrio comercial | ayl bahrreeoa koamehrthyahl |
| castle | el castillo | ayl kahsteelyoa |
| catacombs | las catacumbas | lahss kahtahkoombahss |
| cathedral | la catedral | lah kahtaydrahl |
| cemetery | el cementerio | ayl thaymayntayryoa |
| church | la iglesia | lah eeglayssyah |
| circus | el circo | ayl theerkoa |
| city centre | el centro de la ciudad | ayl thayntroa day lah thyoodhahdh |
| city walls | las murallas | lahss moorahlyahss |
| concert hall | la sala de conciertos | lah sahlah day konthyehrtoass |
| convent | el convento | ayl konbayntoa |
| convention hall | el palacio de convenciones | ayl pahlahthyoa day konbaynthyonayss |
| court house | el palacio de justicia | ayl pahlahthyoa day khoosteethyah |
| docks | el muelle | ayl mwaylyay |
| downtown area | el centro de la ciudad | ayl thayntroa day lah thyoodhahdh |
| exhibition | la exhibición | lah ehkseebheethyon |
| factory | la fábrica | lah fahbreekah |
| fortress | la fortaleza/el alcázar | lah fortahlaythah/ayl ahlkahthahr |
| fountain | la fuente | lah fwayntay |
| gallery | la galería | lah gahlayreeah |
| gardens | los jardines | loss khahrdeenayss |
| harbour | el puerto | ayl pwayrtoa |
| lake | el lago | ayl lahgoa |
| market | el mercado | ayl mehrkahdhoa |
| monastery | el monasterio | ayl moanahstayryoa |
| monument | el monumento | ayl moanoomayntoa |
| mosque | la mezquita | lah maythkeetah |
| museum | el museo | ayl moossayoa |

FOR ASKING THE WAY, see page 144

| old city | la ciudad vieja | lah thyoodhahdh byaykhah |
| opera house | el teatro de la ópera | ayl tayahtroa day lah oapayrah |
| palace | el palacio | ayl pahlahthyoa |
| park | el parque | ayl pahrkay |
| parliament building | el edificio de las Cortes | ayl aydheefeethyoa day lahss kortayss |
| presidential palace | la residencia presidencial | lah rehsseedhaynthyah praysseedhaynthyahl |
| river | el río | ayl reeoa |
| ruins | las ruinas | lahss rweenahss |
| shopping centre | el centro comercial | ayl thayntroa koamayrthyahl |
| stadium | el estadio | ayl aystahdhyoa |
| statue | la estatua | lah aystahtwah |
| stock exchange | la bolsa | lah bolsah |
| synagogue | la sinagoga | lah seenahgoagah |
| tomb | la tumba | lah toombah |
| tower | la torre | lah torreh |
| university | la universidad | lah ooneebhehrseedhahdh |
| zoo | el zoológico | ayl thoalokheekoa |

## Admission

| Is... open on Sundays? | ¿Está... abierto los domingos? | aystah...ahbhyayrtoa loss doameengoass |
| When does it open? | ¿Cuándo lo abren? | kwahndoa loa ahbrayn |
| When does it close? | ¿Cuándo lo cierran? | kwahndoa loa thyayrrahn |
| How much is the entrance fee? | ¿Cuánto vale la entrada? | kwahntoa bahlay lah ayntrahdhah |
| Is there any reduction for students? | ¿Hay algún descuento para estudiantes? | igh ahlgoon dayskwayntoa pahrah aystoodhyahntayss |
| Have you a guide book (in English)? | ¿Tiene usted una guía (en inglés)? | tyaynay oostaydh oonah geeah (ayn eenglayss) |
| Can I buy a catalogue? | ¿Puedo comprar un catálogo? | pwaydhoa komprahr oon kahtahloagoa |
| Is it all right to take pictures? | ¿Se pueden tomar fotografías? | say pwaydhayn toamahr foatoagrahfeeahss |

| ENTRADA LIBRE | ADMISSION FREE |
| PROHIBIDO TOMAR FOTOGRAFIAS | NO CAMERAS ALLOWED |

## Who—What—When?

| | | |
|---|---|---|
| What's that building? | **¿Qué es ese edificio?** | kay ayss **ay**ssay aydhee**fee**thyoa |
| Who was the...? | **¿Quién fue...?** | kyayn fweh |
| architect | **el arquitecto** | ayl ahrkee**tehk**toa |
| artist | **el artista** | ayl ahr**tees**tah |
| painter | **el pintor** | ayl peen**tor** |
| sculptor | **el escultor** | ayl ayskool**tor** |
| Who painted that picture? | **¿Quién pintó ese cuadro?** | kyayn peen**toa** **ay**ssay **kwah**droa |
| When did he live? | **¿En qué época vivió?** | ayn kay **ay**poakah bee**bhyoa** |
| When was it built? | **¿Cuándo se construyó?** | **kwahn**doa say konstroo**yoa** |
| Where's the house where...lived? | **¿Dónde está la casa en que vivió...?** | **doan**day ays**tah** lah **kah**ssah ayn kay bee**bhyoa** |
| We're interested in... | **Nos interesa(n)...** | noss eentay**rays**sah(n) |
| antiques | **las antigüedades** | lahss ahnteegwee-**dhah**dhayss |
| archaeology | **la arqueología** | lah ahrkayoaloa**khee**ah |
| art | **el arte** | ayl **ahr**tay |
| botany | **la botánica** | lah boa**tah**neekah |
| ceramics | **la cerámica** | lah thay**rah**meekah |
| coins | **las monedas** | lahss moa**nay**dhahss |
| crafts | **la artesanía** | lah ahrtayssah**nee**ah |
| fine arts | **las bellas artes** | lahss **bay**lyahss **ahr**tayss |
| furniture | **los muebles** | loss **mway**blayss |
| geology | **la geología** | lah khayoaloa**khee**ah |
| history | **la historia** | lah ees**toa**ryah |
| medicine | **la medicina** | lah maydee**thee**nah |
| music | **la música** | lah **moos**seekah |
| natural history | **la historia natural** | lah ees**toa**ryah nahtoo**rahl** |
| ornithology | **la ornitología** | lah oarneetoaloa**khee**ah |
| painting | **la pintura** | lah peen**too**rah |
| pottery | **la alfarería** | lah ahlfahray**ree**ah |
| prehistory | **la prehistoria** | lah prayees**toa**ryah |
| sculpture | **la escultura** | lah ayskool**too**rah |
| zoology | **la zoología** | lah thoaloa**khee**ah |
| Where's the... department? | **¿Dónde está el departamento de...?** | **doan**day ays**tah** ayl daypahrtah**mayn**toa day |

## Just the adjective you've been looking for...

| It's... | Es... | ayss |
|---|---|---|
| amazing | **asombroso** | ahssoambroassoa |
| awful | **horrible** | orreeblay |
| beautiful | **hermoso** | ayrmoassoa |
| gloomy | **lúgubre** | loogoobray |
| impressive | **impresionante** | eemprayssyoanahntay |
| interesting | **interesante** | eentayrayssahntay |
| magnificent | **magnífico** | mahgneefeekoa |
| monumental | **monumental** | moanoomayntahl |
| overwhelming | **abrumador** | ahbroomahdhor |
| sinister | **siniestro** | seenyaystroa |
| strange | **extraño** | aykstrahñoa |
| superb | **soberbio** | soabhehrbyoa |
| terrible | **terrible** | tehrreeblay |
| terrifying | **aterrador** | ahtehrrahdhor |
| tremendous | **tremendo** | traymayndoa |
| ugly | **feo** | fehoa |

## Religious services

Predominantly Roman Catholic, Spain is rich in cathedrals and churches worth visiting. Most are open to the public except, of course, during mass. If you're interested in taking pictures, you should obtain permission first. Shorts and backless dresses are definitely out when visiting churches.

| Is there a / an...<br>near here? | ¿Hay una... cerca<br>de aquí? | igh oonah...therkah day<br>ahkee |
|---|---|---|
| Catholic / Protestant<br>church | **iglesia católica/<br>protestante** | eeglayssyah kahtoaleekah/<br>proataystahntay |
| synagogue | **sinagoga** | seenahgoagah |
| mosque | **mezquita** | maythkeetah |
| At what time is...? | ¿A qué hora es...? | ah kay oarah ayss |
| mass | **la misa** | lah meessah |
| the service | **el servicio** | ayl sehrbeethyoa |
| Where can I find a...<br>who speaks English? | ¿Dónde puedo<br>encontrar un... que<br>hable inglés? | doanday pwaydhoa<br>aynkontrahr oon...kay<br>ahblay eenglayss |
| priest / minister /<br>rabbi | **sacerdote/ministro/<br>rabino** | sahthehrdoatay/mee-<br>neestroa/rahbheenoa |

SIGHTSEEING

# Relaxing

### Cinema (Movies) – Theatre

You can expect to see a feature film and a newsreel, perhaps a short documentary and numerous commercials. Double features are popular in smaller cinemas. Most films are dubbed in Spanish. The first showing usually starts around 2 p.m. in cities but at 4 elsewhere. An intermission precedes the showing of the main film. Sometimes there are only two showings in the evening—at 7 and 10.30 or 11 p.m.; for these advance booking is advisable. There are numerous open-air cinemas, especially in Andalusia.

Curtain time at the theatre is at 7 and 10.30 or 11 p.m. There are daily performances but a few theatres close one day a week.

You can find out what's playing from the newspapers and billboards or from magazines like "This Week in…"

| | | |
|---|---|---|
| Have you a copy of "This Week in…"? | ¿Tiene usted una cartelera de espectáculos? | tyaynay oostaydh oonah kahrtaylayrah day ayspehktahkooloass |
| What's on at the cinema tonight? | ¿Qué ponen en el cine esta noche? | kay poanehn ayn ayl theenay aystah noachay |
| What's playing at the…theatre? | ¿Qué ponen en el teatro…? | kay poanehn ayn ayl tayahtroa |
| What sort of play is it? | ¿Qué clase de obra de teatro es? | kay klahssay day oabrah day tayahtroa ayss |
| Who is it by? | ¿Quién es el autor? | kyayn ayss ayl owtor |
| At what theatre is that new play by… being performed? | ¿En qué teatro están poniendo esta nueva obra de…? | ayn kay tayahtroa aystahn poanyayndoa aystah nwaybhah oabrah day |
| Where's that new film by…being shown? | ¿Dónde ponen esa nueva película de…? | doanday poanehn ayssah nwaybhah payleekoolah day |

| Who's in it? | ¿Quién actúa? | kyayn ahktooah |
| Who's playing the lead? | ¿Quién es el protagonista? | kyayn ayss ayl proatahgoaneestah |
| Who's the director? | ¿Quién es el director? | kyayn ayss ayl deerehktor |
| Can you recommend a...? | ¿Puede recomendarme...? | pwaydhay rehkoamayndahrmay |
| film | una película | oonah payleekoolah |
| comedy | una comedia | oonah koamaydhyah |
| drama | un drama | oon drahmah |
| musical | una obra musical | oonah oabrah moosseekahl |
| revue | una revista | oonah rehbheestah |
| thriller | una obra de intriga | oonah oabrah day eentreegah |
| Western | una película del Oeste | oonah payleekoolah dayl oaaystay |
| What time does the show begin? | ¿A qué hora empieza la función? | ah kay oarah aympyaythah lah foonthyon |
| What time does the show end? | ¿A qué hora termina la función? | ah kay oarah tayrmeenah lah foonthyon |
| What time does the first evening performance start? | ¿A qué hora empieza la primera función de noche? | ah kay oarah aympyaythah lah preemehrah foonthyon day noachay |
| Are there any tickets for tonight? | ¿Quedan localidades para esta noche? | kaydhahn loakahleedhahdhayss pahrah aystah noachay |
| How much are the tickets? | ¿Cuánto valen las localidades? | kwahntoa bahlayn lahss loakahleedhahdhayss |
| I want to reserve 2 tickets for the show on Friday evening. | Quiero reservar 2 localidades para la función del viernes por la noche. | kyayroa rayssayrbahr 2 loakahleedhahdhayss pahrah lah foonthyon dayl byayrnayss por lah noachay |
| Can I have a ticket for the matinée on Tuesday? | ¿Me puede dar una localidad para la sesión de tarde del martes? | may pwaydhay dahr oonah loakahleedhahdh pahrah lah sayssyon day tahrday dayl mahrtayss |
| I want a seat in the stalls (orchestra). | Quiero una localidad de platea. | kyayroa oonah loakahleedhahdh day plahtayah |
| Not too far back. | No muy atrás. | noa mwee ahtrahss |
| Somewhere in the middle. | En algún lugar en el medio. | ayn ahlgoon loogar ayn ayl maydhoa |

| How much are the seats in the circle (mezzanine)? | ¿Cuánto valen las localidades de anfiteatro? | kwahntoa bahlayn lahss loakahleedhahdhayss day ahnfeetayahtroa |
| May I please have a programme? | ¿Me da un programa, por favor? | may dah oon proagrahmah por fahbhor |
| Can I check this coat? | ¿Puedo dejar este abrigo en el guardarropa? | pwaydhoa daykhahr aystay ahbreegoa ayn ayl gwahrdahrroapah |

---

| Lo siento, las localidades están agotadas. | I'm sorry, we're sold out. |
| Sólo quedan unos cuantos asientos en el anfiteatro. | There are only a few seats left in the circle (mezzanine). |
| ¿Puedo ver su entrada? | May I see your ticket? |
| Este es su sitio. | This is your seat. |

---

RELAXING

## Opera—Ballet—Concert

| Where's the opera house? | ¿Dónde está el Teatro de la Opera? | doanday aystah ayl tayahtroa day lah oapehrah |
| Where's the concert hall? | ¿Dónde está la Sala de Conciertos? | doanday aystah lah sahlah day konthyayrtoass |
| What's on at the opera tonight? | ¿Qué ópera ponen esta noche? | kay oapehrah poanehn aystah noachay |
| Who's singing? | ¿Quién canta? | kyayn kahntah |
| Who's dancing? | ¿Quién baila? | kyayn bighlah |
| What time does the programme start? | ¿A qué hora empieza el programa? | ah kay oarah aympyaythah ayl proagrahmah |
| What orchestra is playing? | ¿Qué orquestra toca? | kay oarkaystrah toakah |
| What are they playing? | ¿Qué tocan? | kay toakahn |
| Who's the conductor? | ¿Quién es el director? | kyayn ayss ayl deerehktor |

## Night-clubs

Night-clubs—with dinner, dancing and a floor show—are found only in major cities and popular spas. But you'll certainly want to experience the informal atmosphere of a *bodega* or *taberna*. Some of them are found in candlelit cellars or in bars where a tiny space has been set aside for entertainment. While sipping a sherry or Spanish brandy, you might watch fiery flamenco dancing or listen to melancholy guitar music.

In holiday resorts along the coast, a lot of *bodegas* are made for the tourist trade; entertainment may be keyed to appeal to foreigners who'll pay high prices for it. But ask around for good *bodegas* and *tabernas* for a more authentic style of singing, dancing and music that the Spaniards enjoy.

| | | |
|---|---|---|
| Can you recommend a good night-club? | ¿Puede recomendarme una buena sala de fiestas? | pwaydhay raykoamayndahrmay oonah bwaynah sahlah day fyaystahss |
| Is there a floor show? | ¿Hay atracciones? | igh ahtrahkthyonayss |
| What time does the floor show start? | ¿A qué hora empiezan las atracciones? | ah kay oarah aympyaythahn lahss ahtrahkthyonayss |
| Is evening attire necessary? | ¿Se necesita traje de noche? | say naythaysseetah trahkhay day noachay |

## And once inside...

| | | |
|---|---|---|
| A table for 2, please. | Una mesa para 2, por favor. | oonah mayssah pahrah 2 por fahbhor |
| My name's...I reserved a table for 4. | Mi nombre es...He reservado una mesa para 4. | mee noambray ayss...ay rayssehrbahdhoa oonah mayssah pahrah 4 |
| I telephoned you earlier. | Le he telefoneado antes. | lay ay taylayfoanehahdhoa ahntayss |
| We haven't got a reservation. | No hemos reservado. | noa aymoass rayssehrbahdhoa |

## Dancing

| | | |
|---|---|---|
| Where can we go dancing? | ¿Dónde podemos ir a bailar? | doanday poadhaymoass eer ah bighlahr |
| Is there a discotheque in town? | ¿Hay alguna discoteca en la ciudad? | igh ahlgoonah deeskoatay-kah ayn lah thyoodhahdh |
| There's a dance at the... | Hay un baile en... | igh oon bighlay ayn |
| Would you like to dance? | ¿Quiere usted bailar? | kyayray oostaydh bighlahr |
| May I have this dance? | ¿Me permite este baile? | may payrmeetay aystay bighlay |

## Do you happen to play...?

On a rainy day, this page may solve your problems.

| | | |
|---|---|---|
| Do you happen to play chess? | ¿Juega usted al ajedrez? | khwaygah oostaydh ahl ahkhaydrayth |
| I'm afraid I don't. | Me temo que no. | may tehmoa kay noa |
| No, but I'll give you a game of draughts (checkers). | No, pero podría jugar a las damas. | noa pehroa poadreeah khoogahr ah lahss dahmahss |
| king | el rey | ayl ray |
| queen | la reina | lah raynah |
| castle (rook) | la torre | lah torreh |
| bishop | el alfil | ayl ahlfeel |
| knight | el caballo | ayl kahbhahlyoa |
| pawn | el peón | ayl pehon |
| Checkmate! | ¡Jaque mate! | khahkay mahtay |
| Do you play cards? | ¿Juega usted a las cartas? | khwaygah oostaydh ah lahss kahrtahss |
| bridge | el bridge | ayl "bridge" |
| canasta | la canasta | lah kahnahstah |
| whist | el whist | ayl "whist" |
| pontoon (21) | el veintiuno | ayl baynteeoonoa |
| poker | el póker | ayl pokehr |
| ace | el as | ayl ahss |
| king | el rey | ayl ray |
| queen | la dama | lah dahmah |
| jack | la sota | lah sotah |
| joker | el comodín | ayl koamoadheen |

FOR NUMBERS, see page 175

RELAXING

| hearts | **corazones** | korah**thoa**nayss |
| diamonds | **diamantes** | dyah**mahn**tayss |
| clubs | **tréboles** | treh**bhoa**layss |
| spades | **picos** | **pee**koass |

In provincial Spain, people might only know the Spanish deck of cards which is somewhat different from ours. Cards are usually numbered from one to seven. The queen is replaced by *el caballo* (ayl kah**bhah**lyoa—the knight), but otherwise the names of the cards are the same as ours. The suits of hearts, diamonds, clubs and spades are replaced by the following designs:

  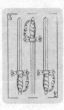 

**copas** (**koa**panss)  **bastos** (bahs**toass**)  **espadas** (ays**pah**dhahss)  **oros** (**oa**roass)

### Bullfight

The *corrida* (literally "running of the bulls") possibly dates back to the Romans. The sport will either fascinate you or appal you.

To understand the Spaniard's appreciation of the *corrida,* you'll have to concede that most cattle do, indeed, spend their lives being fattened up for slaughter. To a Spaniard, a bullfight is not a choice of life and death for the bull. It is simply an opportunity for it to die heroically. The bull will die. The question is how much courage and strength it will show in facing certain death.

In some ways the spectacle resembles a ballet. There are colourful moments when the procession *(paseo)* arrives. The entry of the bull into the arena is a moment of high suspense. The movements of cape and bullfighter are graceful and precise.

The *matador* (Bizet mistakenly termed him *toreador*) and his team of assistants goad the bull so as to assess its reactions to the cape. A *picador* weakens the bull by piercing its neck muscles with a lance.

A *banderillero* then confronts the animal. At great peril, he thrusts three sets of barbed sticks or darts between its shoulder blades. Throughout each stage of the performance the Spanish crowd will be watching critically for the finer points—weighing the fearlessness of bull and man, and the *matador's* skill as he executes a series of dangerous passes.

You may well find the whole performance cruel. Should death be a public spectacle? Disturbing, too, is the treatment of the *picador's* horse. Although protected by padding, he catches the repeated fury of the bull's charge and horns. The horse takes this in silence, incidentally, because his vocal cords have been cut.

You'll be asked whether you want a seat in the sun or shade *(sol o sombra)*. Be sure to specify *sombra,* for the Spanish sun is hot. Rent a cushion *(almohadilla)* for the hard concrete stands.

Photographers should not waste all their films on the first bull, since there are six contests in an afternoon. Wait for action to occur close to your seat. This will provide far more dramatic shots than any taken at a distance.

The *aficionados* show their approval by a vigorous waving of handkerchiefs. The judge awards the bullfighter one ear for a good fight, two for an outstanding contest. The tail is reserved for a really great performance. The *matador* circles the ring once or twice to acknowledge the tributes of the crowd.

| I'd like to see a bullfight. | **Quisiera ver una corrida.** | keessyayrah behr oonah korreedhah |
| I want a seat in the shade / in the sun. | **Quisiera una localidad en la sombra / al sol.** | keessyayrah oonah loakah-leedhahdh ayn lah soambrah / ahl sol |
| I'd like to rent a cushion. | **Quisiera alquilar una almohadilla.** | keessyayrah ahlkeelahr oonah ahlmoaahdheelyah |

## Other sports

Football (soccer) and *pelota* are as popular in Spain as bull-fighting. For an exciting afternoon, go and see one of the world-renowned Spanish football teams, such as Real Madrid, in action.

*Pelota* is similar to handball but instead of a glove, the players wear a curved wicker basket *(cesta)*. The ball *(pelota)* is hard and covered with goatskin. It can be played off the back and side walls as well as the front. Caught in the *cesta,* and hurled at the wall with great force, it bounces with extraordinary speed. Usually played in the late afternoon or evening, *pelota* is well worth watching.

In Latin America, the game is known as *jai alai* (the Basque word for the sport). The Basques, from the north of Spain, may have invented the game themselves. However, some think it was played by the Mayas or Aztecs and was brought back to Spain by the *conquistadores.*

In spring and fall, there's good horse racing in Madrid, San Sebastian and Seville. Besides, facilities abound to go fishing—even deep-sea fishing—hunting, golfing, swimming, surfing or play tennis.

Though one wouldn't think of going to Spain to ski, you can don your ski togs from December to April in the Catalonian Pyrenees, near Madrid and in the Sierra Nevada near Granada.

RELAXING

| Is there a football (soccer) match anywhere today? | ¿Hay algún partido de fútbol hoy? | igh ahlgoon pahrteedhoa day footbol hoy |
| Who's playing? | ¿Quiénes juegan? | kyaynayss khwaygahn |
| Where's the nearest golf course? | ¿Dónde está el campo de golf más cercano? | doanday aystah ayl kahmpoa day goalf mahss thehrkahnoa |
| Can we hire (rent) clubs? | ¿Podemos alquilar los palos? | poadhaymoass ahlkeelahr loss pahloass |
| Where are the tennis courts? | ¿Dónde están las pistas de tennis? | doanday aystahn lahss peestahss day tayneess |
| Can I hire rackets? | ¿Puedo alquilar raquetas? | pwaydhoa ahlkeelahr rahkaytahss |
| What's the charge per...? | ¿Cuánto cuesta por...? | kwahntoa kwaystah por |
| day / round / hour | día / juego / hora | deeah / khwaygoa / oarah |
| Where's the nearest race course (track)? | ¿Dónde está la pista de carreras más cercana? | doanday aystah lah peestah day kahrrehrahss mahss thehrkahnah |
| What's the admission charge? | ¿Cuánto vale la entrada? | kwahntoa bahlay lah ayntrahdhah |
| Is there a swimming pool here? | ¿Hay una piscina aquí? | igh oonah peestheenah ahkee |
| Is it open-air / indoors / heated? | ¿Está al aire libre / es cubierta / climatizada? | aystah ahl ighray leebray / ayss koobyayrtah / kleemahteethahdhah |
| Can one swim in the lake / river? | ¿Puede uno nadar en el lago / río? | pwaydhay oonoa nahdhahr ayn ayl lahgoa / reeoa |
| Can you get me a couple of tickets? | ¿Puede conseguirme algunas entradas? | pwaydhay konsaygeermay ahlgoonahss ayntrahdhahss |
| I'd like to see a pelota match. | Quisiera ver un partido de pelota. | keessyayrah behr oon pahrteedhoa day payloatah |

## On the beach

| | | |
|---|---|---|
| Is it safe for swimming? | ¿Se puede nadar sin peligro? | say pwaydhay nahdhahr seen pehleegroa |
| Is there a lifeguard? | ¿Hay vigilante? | igh beekheelahntay |
| Is it safe for children? | ¿Es segura para los niños? | ayss sehgoorah pahrah loss neeñoass |
| It's very calm. | Está muy tranquila. | aystah mwee trahnkeelah |
| There are some big waves. | Hay algunas olas muy grandes. | igh ahlgoonahss oalahss mwee grahndayss |
| Are there any dangerous currents? | ¿Hay alguna corriente peligrosa? | igh ahlgoonah korryayntay pehleegroassah |
| What time is high/low tide? | ¿A qué hora es la marea alta/baja? | ah kay oarah ayss lah mahrehah ahltah/bahkhah |
| What's the temperature of the water? | ¿Cuál es la temperatura del agua? | kwahl ayss lah taympayrahtoorah dayl ahgwah |
| I want to hire a/an... | Quiero alquilar... | kyayroa ahlkeelahr |
| air mattress | un colchón neumático | oon koalchon nayoomahteekoa |
| bathing hut | una cabina | oonah kahbheenah |
| deck-chair | una silla de lona | oonah seelyah day loanah |
| skin-diving equipment | un equipo para natación submarina | oon aykeepoa pahrah nahtahthyon soobmahreenah |
| sunshade | una sombrilla | oonah soambreelyah |
| surfboard | una plancha de deslizamiento | oonah plahnchah day daysleethiahmyayntoa |
| some water skis | unos esquís acuáticos | oonoass ayskeess ahkwahteekoass |
| Where can I rent...? | ¿Dónde puedo alquilar...? | doanday pwaydhoa ahlkeelahr |
| a canoe | una canoa | oonah kahnoaah |
| a motor boat | una motora | oonah moatoarah |
| a rowing-boat | una barca | oonah bahrkah |
| a sailing-boat | un velero | oon baylehroa |
| What's the charge per hour? | ¿Cuánto cobran por hora? | kwahntoa koabrahn por oarah |

---

| | |
|---|---|
| **PLAYA PARTICULAR** | PRIVATE BEACH |
| **PROHIBIDO BAÑARSE** | NO BATHING |

# Camping—Countryside

In some parts of Spain, camping isn't allowed without a permit. However, there are many authorized camping sites with excellent facilities. Camping and sleeping on the beach isn't recommended.

For information about youth hostels and similar accommodation, apply to your national youth hostel organization or to student travel offices.

| Can we camp here? | ¿Podemos acampar aquí? | poadhaymoass ahkahmpahr ahkee |
| Where can one camp for the night? | ¿Dónde se puede acampar por la noche? | doanday say pwaydhay ahkahmpahr por lah noachay |
| Is there a camping site near here? | ¿Hay algún camping cerca de aquí? | igh algoon kahmpeeng thehrkah day ahkee |
| May we camp in your field? | ¿Podemos acampar en su terreno? | poadhaymoass ahkahmpahr ayn soo tehrraynoa |
| Can we park our caravan (trailer) here? | ¿Podemos estacionar nuestra caravana aquí? | poadhaymoass aystahthyonahr nwaystrah kahrahbhahnah ahkee |
| Is this an official camping site? | ¿Es éste un camping oficial? | ayss aystay oon kahmpeeng oafeethyahl |
| May we light a fire? | ¿Podemos encender una hoguera? | poadhaymoass aynthayndehr oonah oagehrah |
| Is there drinking water? | ¿Hay agua potable? | igh ahgwah poatahblay |
| What are the facilities? | ¿Cuáles son los servicios? | kwahlayss son loss sehrbeethyoass |
| Are there shopping facilities on the site? | ¿Hay tiendas en el recinto? | igh tyayndahss ayn ayl raytheentoa |
| Are there...? | ¿Hay...? | igh |
| baths | baños | bahñoass |
| showers | duchas | doochahss |
| toilets | retretes | raytrehtayss |

| What's the charge...? | ¿Cuál es el precio...? | kwahl ayss ayl praythyoa |
| per day | por día | por deeah |
| per person | por persona | por pehrsoanah |
| for a car | por coche | por koachay |
| for a tent | por tienda | por tyayndah |
| for a caravan (trailer) | por caravana | por kahrahbhahnah |

| Is there a youth hostel near here? | ¿Hay algún albergue juvenil cerca de aquí? | igh ahlgoon ahlbehrgay khoobhayneel thehrkah day ahkee |

| Do you know anyone who can put us up for the night? | ¿Sabe usted de alguien que pudiera alojarnos por la noche? | sahbhay oostaydh day ahlgyayn kay poodhyayrah ahloakhahrnoass por lah noachay |

| PROHIBIDO ACAMPAR | PROHIBIDO ACAMPAR CON CARAVANA |
| NO CAMPING | NO CARAVANS (TRAILERS) |

## Landmarks

| barn | el granero | ayl grahnayroa |
| beach | la playa | lah plahyah |
| bridge | el puente | ayl pwayntay |
| brook | el arroyo | ayl ahrroayoa |
| building | el edificio | ayl aydheefeethyoa |
| canal | el canal | ayl kahnahl |
| castle | el castillo | ayl kahsteelyoa |
| church | la iglesia | lah eeglayssyah |
| cliff | el acantilado | ayl ahkahnteelahdhoa |
| copse | el matorral | ayl mahtorrahl |
| crossroads | el cruce | ayl kroothay |
| farm | la granja | lah grahnkhah |
| field | el campo | ayl kahmpoa |
| footpath | el sendero | ayl sayndayroa |
| forest | el bosque | ayl boaskay |
| fortress | la fortaleza | lah fortahlaythah |
| hamlet | el caserío | ayl kassayreeoa |
| heath | el brezal | ayl brehthahl |
| highway | la autopista | lah owtoapeestah |
| hill | la colina | lah koaleenah |
| house | la casa | lah kahssah |
| hut | la cabaña | lah kahbhahñah |
| inn | la fonda | lah foandah |
| lake | el lago | ayl lahgoa |

CAMPING

| | | |
|---|---|---|
| marsh | el pantano | ayl pahntahnoa |
| moorland | el páramo | ayl pahrahmoa |
| mountain | la montaña | lah moantahñah |
| mountain range | la cadena montañosa | lah kahdhaynah moantahñoassah |
| path | la senda | lah sayndah |
| peak | el pico | ayl peekoa |
| pond | la charca | lah chahrkah |
| pool | el estanque | ayl ehstahnkay |
| railway track | la vía de ferrocarril | lah beeah day fehrroakahrreel |
| river | el río | ayl reeoa |
| road | la carretera | lah kahrraytayrah |
| sea | el mar | ayl mahr |
| spring | el manantial | ayl mahnahntyahl |
| stream | la corriente | lah koarryayntay |
| swamp | el pantano | ayl pahntahnoa |
| tower | la torre | lah toarreh |
| track | el camino | ayl kahmeenoa |
| tree | el árbol | ayl ahrbol |
| valley | el valle | ayl bahlyay |
| village | la villa/el pueblo | lah beelyah/ayl pwaybloa |
| vineyard | el viñedo | ayl beeñaydhoa |
| waterfall | la cascada | lah kahskahdhah |
| watermill | el molino de agua | ayl moaleenoa day ahgwah |
| water tower | la torre de agua | lah toarreh day ahgwah |
| well | el pozo | ayl poathoa |
| windmill | el molino de viento | ayl moaleenoa day byayntoa |
| wood | el bosque | ayl boaskay |
| What's the name of that river? | ¿Cómo se llama ese río? | koamoa say lyahmah ayssay reeoa |
| How high is that mountain? | ¿Qué altura tiene esa montaña? | kay ahltoorah tyaynay ayssah moantahñah |
| How far is the next town? | ¿A qué distancia estamos de la próxima ciudad? | ah kay deestahnthyah ays-tahmoass day lah prok-seemah thyoodhahdh |
| Where does this road lead to? | ¿Adónde lleva esta carretera? | ahdoanday lyaybhah aystah kahrrehtayrah |

...and if you're tired of walking, you can always try hitch-hiking, though you may have to wait a long time for a lift:

| | | |
|---|---|---|
| Can you give me a lift to...? | ¿Puede llevarme a...? | pwaydhay lyaybhahrmay ah |

FOR ASKING THE WAY, see page 144

# Making friends

## Introductions

Here are a few phrases to get you started:

| | | |
|---|---|---|
| How do you do? | **Encantado de conocerle/conocerla.** | aynkahntahdhoa day koanoathehrlay/ koanoathehrlah |
| How are you? | **¿Cómo está usted?** | koamoa aystah oostaydh |
| Fine, thanks. And you? | **Bien, gracias. ¿Y usted?** | byayn grahthyahss. ee oostaydh |
| May I introduce Miss Philips? | **Quiero presentarle a Miss Philips.** | kyayroa prayssayntahrlay ah Miss Philips |
| I'd like you to meet a friend of mine. | **Le voy a presentar a un amigo mío.** | lay boy ah praysoonyntahr ah oon ahmeegoa meeoa |
| John, this is.. | **Juan, te presento a...** | khwahn tay prayssayntoa ah |
| My name's... | **Me llamo...** | may lyahmoa |
| Glad to know you. | **Tanto gusto** | tahntoa goostoa |

## Follow-up

| | | |
|---|---|---|
| How long have you been here? | **¿Cuánto tiempo lleva usted aquí?** | kwahntoa tyaympoa lyaybhah oostaydh ahkee |
| We've been here a week. | **Llevamos aquí una semana.** | lyaybhahmoass ahkee oonah saymahnah |
| Is this your first visit? | **¿Es la primera vez que viene?** | ayss lah preemayrah behth kay byaynay |
| No, we came here last year. | **No, vinimos el año pasado.** | noa beeneemoass ayl ahñoa pahssahdhoa |
| Are you on your own? | **¿Ha venido usted solo/sola?** | ah bayneedhoa oostaydh soaloa/soalah |
| I'm with... | **Estoy con...** | aystoy kon |
| my husband | **mi marido** | mee mahreedhoa |
| my wife | **mi mujer** | mee mookhehr |
| my family | **mi familia** | mee fahmeelyah |
| my parents | **mis padres** | meess pahdrayss |
| some friends | **unos amigos** | oonoass ahmeegoass |

| | | |
|---|---|---|
| Are you enjoying your stay? | ¿Está disfrutando de su estancia? | aystah deesfrootahndoa day soo aystahnthyah |
| Yes, I like...very much. | Sí, me gusta mucho... | see may goostah moochoa |
| Where do you come from? | ¿De dónde es usted? | day doanday ayss oostaydh |
| What part of...do you come from? | ¿De qué parte de... es usted? | day kay pahrtay day... ayss oostaydh |
| I'm from... | Soy de... | soy day |
| Where are you staying? | ¿Dónde se hospeda? | doanday say ospehdhah |
| I'm a student. | Soy estudiante. | soy aystoodhyahntay |
| We're here on holiday. | Estamos aquí de vacaciones. | aystahmoass ahkee day bahkahthyonayss |
| I'm here on a business trip. | Estoy aquí en viaje de negocios. | aystoy ahkee ayn byah-khay day naygoathyoass |
| What's your occupation? | ¿Cuál es su ocupación? | kwahl ayss soo oakoopahthyon |
| We hope to see you again soon. | Esperamos verle pronto por aquí. | ayspayrahmoass bayrlay proantoa por ahkee |
| See you later/See you tomorrow. | Hasta luego/Hasta mañana. | ahstah lwaygoa/ahstah mahñahnah |

## The weather

Always a good topic for conversation, in Spain as much as elsewhere. So...

| | | |
|---|---|---|
| What a lovely day! | ¡Qué día tan bueno! | kay deeah tahn bwaynoa |
| What awful weather! | ¡Qué tiempo más malo! | kay tyaympoa mahss mahloa |
| Isn't it cold/hot today? | ¿Qué frío/calor hace hoy, verdad? | kay freeoa/kahlor ahthay oy behrdahdh |
| Is it usually as warm as this? | ¿Hace normalmente este calor? | ahthay noarmahlmayntay ahstay kahlor |
| Do you think it'll ...tomorrow? | ¿Cree usted que... mañana? | krayeh oostaydh kay... mahñahnah |
| rain/snow clear up/be sunny | lloverá/nevará hará mejor/hará sol | lyoabhayrah/naybhahrah ahrah mehkhor/ahrah sol |

## Invitations

| | | |
|---|---|---|
| My wife and I would like you to dine with us on... | Mi mujer y yo quisiéramos invitarle a cenar el... | mee mookhehr ee yoa keessyayrahmoass eenbeetahrlay ah thaynahr ayl |
| Can you come to dinner tomorrow night? | ¿Puede usted venir a cenar mañana por la noche? | pwaydhay oostaydh bayneer ah thaynahr mahñahnah por lah noachay |
| Can you come over for cocktails this evening? | ¿Puede usted venir a tomar unas copas esta noche? | pwaydhay oostaydh bayneer ah toamahr oonahss koapahss aystah noachay |
| There's a party. Are you coming? | Hay un guateque. ¿Quiere usted venir? | igh oon gwahtehkay. kyayray oostaydh bayneer |
| That's very kind of you. | Es usted muy amable. | ayss oostaydh mwee ahmahblay |
| Great. I'd love to come. | Estupendo. Me encantaría ir. | aystoopayndoa. may aynkahntahreeah eer |
| What time shall we come? | ¿A qué hora vamos? | ah kay oarah bahmoass |
| May I bring a friend? | ¿Puedo llevar a un amigo? | pwaydhoa lyaybhar ah oon ahmeegoa |
| I'm afraid we've got to go now. | Me temo que debemos marcharnos ahora. | may taymoa kay daybhaymoass mahrchahrnoass ahorah |
| Next time you must come to visit us. | Otro día tienen que venir ustedes a vernos. | oatroa deeah tyaynayn kay bayneer oostaydhayss ah bayrnoass |
| Thanks for the evening. It was great. | Muchas gracias por la velada. Ha sido estupenda. | moochahs grahthyahss por lah baylahdhah. ah seedhoa aystoopayndah |

## Dating

| | | |
|---|---|---|
| Would you like a cigarette? | ¿Quiere usted un cigarrillo? | kyayray oostaydh oon theegahrreelyoa |
| Do you have a light, please? | ¿Tiene usted lumbre, por favor? | tyaynay oostaydh loombray por fahbhor |
| Can I get you a drink? | ¿Quiere usted beber algo? | kyayray oostaydh baybhayr ahlgoa |

| Are you waiting for someone? | ¿Está usted esperando a alguien? | aystah oostaydh ayspay-rahndoa ah ahlgyayn |
| Are you free this evening? | ¿Está usted libre esta tarde? | aystah oostaydh leebray aystah tahrday |
| Would you like to go out with me tonight? | ¿Quisiera usted salir conmigo esta noche? | keessyayrah oostaydh sahleer konmeegoa aystah noachay |
| Would you like to go dancing? | ¿Quisiera usted ir a bailar? | keessyayrah oostaydh eer ah bighlahr |
| I know a good discotheque. | Conozco una buena discoteca. | koanoathkoa oonah bwaynah deeskotaykah |
| Shall we go to the cinema (movies)? | ¿Quiere que vayamos al cine? | kyayray kay bahyahmoass ahl theenay |
| Would you like to go for a drive? | ¿Quiere usted dar un paseo en coche? | kyayray oostaydh dahr oon pahssayoa ayn koachay |
| I'd love to, thank you. | Me encantaría, gracias. | may aynkahntahreeah grahthyahss |
| Where shall we meet? | ¿Dónde nos encontramos? | doanday noss aynkontrahmoss |
| I'll pick you up at your hotel. | La recogeré en su hotel. | lah rehkokhayray ayn soo oatehl |
| I'll call for you at 8 o'clock. | Iré a recogerla a las 8. | eeray ah rehkokkhayrlah ah lahss 8 |
| May I take you home? | ¿Puedo acompañarla hasta su casa? | pwaydhoa ahkoampah-ñahrlah ahstah soo kahssah |
| Can I see you again tomorrow? | ¿Puedo verla mañana? | pwaydhoa bayrlah mañahnah |
| Thank you, it's been a wonderful evening. | Gracias, ha sido una tarde estupenda. | grahthyahss ah seedhoa oonah tahrday aystoo-payndah |
| I've enjoyed myself tremendously. | Lo he pasado muy bien. | loa ay pahssahdhoa mwee byayn |
| What's your telephone number? | ¿Cuál es su número de teléfono? | kwahl ayss soo noomayroa day taylayfoanoa |
| Do you live alone? | ¿Vive usted sola? | beebhay oostaydh soalah |
| What time is your last train? | ¿A qué hora es su último tren? | ah kay oarah ayss soo oolteemoa trayn |

# Shopping guide

This shopping guide is designed to help you find what you want with ease, accuracy and speed. It features:

1. A list of all major shops, stores and services (p. 98)

2. Some general expressions required when shopping to allow you to be specific and selective (p. 100)

3. Full details of the shops and services most likely to concern you. Here you'll find advice, alphabetical lists of items and conversion charts listed under the headings below.

|  |  | Page |
|---|---|---|
| **Bookshop** | books, magazines, newspapers, stationery | 104 |
| **Camping** | camping equipment | 106 |
| **Chemist's (drugstore)** | medicine, first-aid, cosmetics, toilet articles | 108 |
| **Clothing** | clothes, shoes, accessories | 112 |
| **Electrical appliances** | radios, tape-recorders, shavers, records | 119 |
| **Hairdresser's** | barber's, ladies' hairdresser's, beauty salon | 121 |
| **Jeweller's** | jewellery, watches, watch repairs | 123 |
| **Laundry— Dry cleaning** | usual facilities | 126 |
| **Photography** | cameras, accessories, films, developing | 127 |
| **Provisions** | this is confined to basic items required for picnics | 129 |
| **Souvenirs** | souvenirs, gifts, fancy goods | 131 |
| **Tobacconist's** | smoker's supplies | 132 |

## Shops, stores and services

If you have a pretty clear idea of what you want before you set out, then look under the appropriate heading, pick out the article and find a suitable description for it (colour, material, etc.).

Shops in Spain usually open around 9 a.m. and close between 8.00 p.m. and 8.30 p.m. All close for lunch from 1.00 p.m. to 3.30 or 4 p.m. in summer. Few shops are open on Sundays or public holidays.

| Where's the nearest...? | ¿Dónde está... más cercano/cercana? | doanday aystah...mahss thayrkahnoa/thayrkahnah |
|---|---|---|
| antique shop | la tienda de antigüedades | lah tyayndah day ahnteegweedhahdhayss |
| art gallery | la galería de arte | lah gahlayreeah day ahrtay |
| baker's | la panadería | lah pahnahdhayreeah |
| bank | el banco | ayl bahnkoa |
| barber's | la barbería | lah bahrbayreeah |
| beauty salon | el salón de belleza | ayl sahlon day baylyaythah |
| bookshop | la librería | lah leebrayreeah |
| bookstall | el puesto de libros | ayl pwaystoa day leebroass |
| butcher's | la carnicería | lah kahrneethayreeah |
| camera store | la tienda de fotografía | lah tyayndah day foatoagrahfeeah |
| candy store | la bombonería | lah boamboanayreeah |
| chemist's | la farmacia | lah fahrmahthyah |
| cobbler | el zapatero | ayl thahpahtayroa |
| confectioner's | la pastelería | lah pahstaylayreeah |
| dairy | la lechería | lah laychayreeah |
| delicatessen | la mantequería | lah mahntaykayreeah |
| dentist | el dentista | ayl daynteestah |
| department store | los grandes almacenes | loss grahndayss ahlmahthaynayss |
| doctor | el médico | ayl maydeekoa |
| draper's | la pañería | lah pahñayreeah |
| dressmaker's | la modista | lah moadeestah |
| drugstore | la farmacia | lah fahrmahthyah |
| dry cleaner's | la tintorería | lah teentoarayreeah |
| dry goods store | la lencería | lah laynthayreeah |
| fishmonger's | la pescadería | lah payskahdhayreeah |
| florist's | la florería | lah floarayreeah |
| furrier's | la peletería | lah paylaytayreeah |

| green grocer's | la verdulería | lah behrdoolayreeah |
|---|---|---|
| grocery | la tienda | lah **tyayndah** |
| hairdresser's (ladies) | la peluquería | lah paylookayreeah |
| hardware store | la ferretería | lah fehrraytayreeah |
| hat shop | la sombrerería | lah soambrehrayreeah |
| hospital | el hospital | ayl oaspeetahl |
| jeweller | la joyería | lah khoyayreeah |
| laundry | la lavandería | lah lahbhahndayreeah |
| leather-goods store | la tienda de artículos de cuero | lah **tyayndah** day ahrteekooloass day **kwayroa** |
| liquor store | la tienda de licores | lah **tyayndah** day leekoarayss |
| market | el mercado | ayl mehrkahdhoa |
| milliner's | la sombrerería | lah soambrayrayreeah |
| news-stand | el quiosco de periódicos | ayl **kyoskoa** day payryodheekoass |
| off-licence | la tienda de licores | lah **tyayndah** day leekoarayss |
| optician | el óptico | ayl **optookon** |
| pastry shop | la pastelería | lah pahstaylayreeah |
| pawnbroker | la prestamista | lah praystahmeestah |
| photo shop | la tienda de fotografía | lah **tyayndah** day foatoagrahfeeah |
| police station | la comisaría | lah koameessahreeah |
| post-office | la oficina de correos | lah oaffetheenah day korrehoass |
| shirt-maker's | la camisería | lah kahmeessehreeah |
| shoemaker's (repairs) | el zapatero | ayl thahpahtayroa |
| shoe shop | la zapatería | lah thahpahtayreeah |
| souvenir shop | la tienda de objetos de regalo | lah **tyayndah** day oabkhaytoass day raygahloa |
| sporting-goods shop | la tienda de artículos de deportes | lah **tyayndah** day ahrteekooloass day dayportayss |
| stationer's | la papelería | lah pahpaylayreeah |
| supermarket | el supermercado | ayl soopayrmayr**kahd**hoa |
| sweet shop | la bombonería | lah boamboanayreeah |
| tailor | el sastre | ayl **sahs**tray |
| tobacconist's | el estanco | ayl ehstahnkoa |
| toy shop | la juguetería | lah khoogaytayreeah |
| travel agent | la agencia de viajes | lah ah**khay**nthyah day **byah**khayss |
| vegetable store | la verdulería | lah bayrdoolayreeah |
| veterinarian | el veterinario | ayl baytayreenahryoa |
| watchmaker's | la relojería | lah rehlokhayreeah |
| wine merchant's | la tienda de vinos/ la bodega | lah **tyayndah** day beenoass/lah boadhaygah |

### General expressions

Here are some expressions which will be useful to you when you're out shopping:

#### Where?

| | | |
|---|---|---|
| Where's a good...? | ¿Dónde hay un buen/una buena...? | doanday igh oon bwayn/oonah bwaynah |
| Where can I find a...? | ¿Dónde puedo encontrar un/una...? | doanday pwaydhoa aynkoantrahr oon/oonah |
| Where do they sell...? | ¿Dónde venden...? | doanday bayndayn |
| Can you recommend an inexpensive...? | ¿Puede usted recomendarme un...barato? | pwaydhay oostaydh rehkomayndahrmay oon...bahrahtoa |
| Where's the main shopping area? | ¿Dónde está el área de tiendas más importante? | doanday aystah ayl ahrehah day tyayndahss mahss eempoartahntay |
| How far is it from here? | ¿Está muy lejos de aquí? | aystah mwee lehkhoass day ahkee |
| How do I get there? | ¿Cómo puedo llegar allí? | koamoa pwaydhoa lyaygahr ahlyee |

#### Service

| | | |
|---|---|---|
| Can you help me? | ¿Puede usted atenderme? | pwaydhay oostaydh ahtayndayrmay |
| I'm just looking around. | Estoy sólo mirando. | aystoy soaloa meerahndoa |
| I want... | Quiero... | kyayroa |
| Do you have any...? | ¿Tiene usted...? | tyaynay oostaydh |

#### That one

| | | |
|---|---|---|
| Can you show me...? | ¿Puede usted enseñarme...? | pwaydhay oostaydh aynsayñahrmay |
| that/those | ése/ésos | ayssay/ayssoass |
| the one in the window/in the display case | el del escaparate/de la vitrina | ayl dayl ehskahpahrahtay/day lah beetreenah |
| It's over there. | Es allí. | ayss ahlyee |

## Defining the article

| | | |
|---|---|---|
| I'd like a... | **Quisiera un...** | kee**ss**yayrah oon |
| It must be... | **Debe ser...** | day**bh**ay sayr |
| big | **grande** | **grah**nday |
| cheap | **barato** | bah**rah**toa |
| dark | **oscuro** | os**koo**roa |
| good | **bueno** | **bway**noa |
| heavy | **pesado** | pay**ssah**dhoa |
| large | **grande** | **grah**nday |
| light (weight) | **ligero** | lee**khay**roa |
| light (colour) | **claro** | **klah**roa |
| oval | **ovalado** | obhah**lah**dhoa |
| rectangular | **rectangular** | rehktahn**goo**lahr |
| round | **redondo** | ray**dhon**doa |
| small | **pequeño** | pay**kay**ñoa |
| square | **cuadrado** | kwah**drah**dhoa |
| I don't want anything too expensive. | **No quiero algo muy caro.** | noa **kyay**roa **ahl**goa mwee **kah**roa |

## Preference

| | | |
|---|---|---|
| Can you show me some more? | **¿Puede usted enseñarme algo más?** | **pway**dhay oo**stay**dh ayn**say**ñahrmay **ahl**goa mahss |
| Haven't you anything...? | **¿No tiene usted algo...?** | noa **tyay**nay oo**stay**dh **ahl**goa |
| cheaper / better | **más barato / mejor** | mahss bah**rah**toa / **meh**khor |
| larger / smaller | **más grande / más pequeño** | mahss **grah**nday / mahss pay**kay**ñoa |

## How much?

| | | |
|---|---|---|
| How much is this? | **¿Cuánto cuesta esto?** | **kwah**ntoa **kway**stah **ay**stoa |
| I don't understand. | **No entiendo.** | noa ayn**tyay**ndoa |
| Please write it down. | **Escríbamelo, por favor.** | ays**kree**bhahmayloa por fah**bh**or |
| I don't want to spend more than 500 pesetas. | **No quiero gastar más de 500 pesetas.** | noa **kyay**roa gah**stahr** mahss day 500 pay**ssay**tahss |

FOR COLOURS, see page 113

SHOPPING GUIDE

## Decision

| | | |
|---|---|---|
| That's just what I want. | **Eso es justamente lo que quiero.** | ayssoa ayss khoostah-mayntay loa kay kyayroa |
| It's not quite what I want. | **No es realmente lo que quiero.** | noa ayss rehahlmayntay loa kay kyayroa |
| No, I don't like it. | **No, no me gusta.** | noa noa may goostah |
| I'll take it. | **Me lo llevo.** | may loa lyaybhoa |

## Ordering

| | | |
|---|---|---|
| Can you order it for me? | **¿Puede usted encargarlo para mí?** | pwaydhay oostaydh aynkahrgahrloa pahrah mee |
| How long will it take? | **¿Cuánto tardará?** | kwahntoa tahrdahrah |

## Delivery

| | | |
|---|---|---|
| I'll take it with me. | **Me lo llevo.** | may loa lyaybhoa |
| Deliver it to the... Hotel. | **Envíelo al hotel...** | aynbeeayloa ahl oatehl |
| Please send it to this address. | **Por favor, mándelo a estas señas.** | por fahbhor mahndayloa ah aystahss sayñahss |
| Will I have any difficulty with the customs? | **¿Tendré alguna dificultad con la aduana?** | tayndray ahlgoonah deefeekooltahdh kon lah ahdwahnah |

## Paying

| | | |
|---|---|---|
| How much is it? | **¿Cuánto es?** | kwahntoa ayss |
| Can I pay by traveller's cheque? | **¿Puedo pagar con cheque de viajero?** | pwaydhoa pahgahr kon chaykay day byahkhayroa |
| Do you accept dollars / pounds / credit cards? | **¿Acepta usted dólares/libras/ tarjetas de crédito?** | ahthehptah oostaydh doa-lahrayss/leebrahss/tahr-khaytahss day kraydheetoa |
| Haven't you made a mistake in the bill? | **¿No se ha equivocado usted en la cuenta?** | noa say ah aykeebhoa-kahdhoa oostaydh ayn lah kwayntah |
| Will you please wrap it? | **¿Me hace el favor de envolverlo?** | may ahthay ayl fahbhor day aynbolbehrloa |

## Anything else?

| No, thanks, that's all. | **No gracias, eso es todo.** | noa **grahth**yahss **ayss**oa ayss **toa**dhoa |
| Yes, I want... | **Sí, quiero...** | see **kyay**roa |
| Thank you. Good-bye. | **Gracias. Adiós.** | **grahth**yahss. ah**dhyoss** |

## Dissatisfied

| Can you please exchange this? | **¿Podría usted cambiarme esto, por favor?** | poa**dree**ah oos**taydh** kahm**byahr**may **ays**toa por fah**bhor** |
| I want to return this. | **Quiero devolver esto.** | **kyay**roa daybhol**behr ays**toa |
| I'd like a refund. Here's the receipt. | **Quisiera que me devolviesen el dinero. Aquí está el recibo.** | kees**syay**rah kay may daybhol**byays**sayn ayl dee**nay**roa. ah**kee** ays**tah** ayl ray**thee**bhoa |

---

| ¿En qué puedo ayudarle? | Can I help you? |
| ¿Qué desea? | What would you like? |
| ¿Qué... desea? | What... would you like? |
| color / forma calidad / cantidad | colour / shape quality / quantity |
| Lo siento, no lo tenemos. | I'm sorry, we haven't any. |
| Se nos ha agotado. | We're out of stock. |
| ¿Quiere que se lo encarguemos? | Shall we order it for you? |
| ¿Lo llevará consigo o se lo enviamos? | Will you take it with you or shall we send it? |
| ¿Algo más? | Anything else? |
| Son... pesetas, por favor. | That's... pesetas, please. |
| La caja está allí. | The cashier's over there. |

### Bookshop—Stationer's—News-stand

In Spain, bookshops and stationers' are usually separate shops, though the latter will often sell paperbacks. Newspapers and magazines are sold at news-stands.

| | | |
|---|---|---|
| Where's the nearest...? | ¿Dónde está... más cercano/cercana? | doanday aystah...mahss thehrkahnoa/thehrkahnah |
| bookshop | la librería | lah leebrayreeah |
| stationer's | la papelería | lah pahpaylayreeah |
| news-stand | el quiosco de periódicos | ayl kyoskoa day payryodheekoass |
| Where can I buy an English newspaper? | ¿Dónde puedo comprar un periódico inglés? | doanday pwaydhoa komprahr oon payryodheekoa eenglayss |
| I want to buy a/an/some... | Quiero... | kyayroa |
| address book | un librito de direcciones | oon leebreetoa day deerehkthyonayss |
| ball-point pen | un bolígrafo | oon boaleegrahfoa |
| book | un libro | oon leebroa |
| box of paints | una caja de pinturas | oonah kahkhah day peentoorahss |
| carbon paper | papel carbón | pahpehl kahrbon |
| cellophane tape | cinta adhesiva | theentah ahdhaysseebhah |
| crayons | unos carboncillos | oonoas kharboantheelyoass |
| dictionary | un diccionario | oon deekthyoanahryoa |
| Spanish-English | Español-Inglés | ayspahñol-eenglayss |
| drawing paper | papel de dibujo | pahpehl day deebhookhoa |
| drawing pins | chinchetas | cheenchaytahss |
| envelopes | unos sobres | oonoas soabrayss |
| eraser | una goma de borrar | oonah goamah day borrahr |
| exercise book | un cuaderno | oon kwahdhehrnoa |
| file | una carpeta | oonah kahrpaytah |
| fountain pen | una pluma estilográfica | oonah ploomah aysteeloagrahfeekah |
| glue | cola de pegar | koalah day paygahr |
| grammar book | un libro de gramática | con leebroa day grahmahteekah |
| guide book | una guía | oonah geeah |
| ink | tinta | teentah |
| black/red/blue | negra/roja/azul | naygrah/roakhah/ahthool |
| labels | unas etiquetas | oonahss ayteekaytahss |
| magazine | una revista | oonah raybheestah |

| map | un mapa | oon mahpah |
| of the town | de la ciudad | day lah thyoodhahdh |
| road map of... | de carreteras de... | day kahrraytayrahss day |
| newspaper | un periódico | oon payryodheekoa |
| American / English | americano/inglés | ahmayreekahnoa/ eenglayss |
| note book | un cuaderno | oon kwahdhehrnoa |
| note paper | papel de cartas | pahpehl day kahrtahss |
| paperback | una rústica | oonah roosteekah |
| paper napkins | unas servilletas de papel | oonahss sayrbeelyaytahss day pahpehl |
| paste | engrudo | ayngroodhoa |
| pen | una pluma | oonah ploomah |
| pencil | un lápiz | oon lahpeeth |
| pencil sharpener | un sacapuntas | oon sahkahpoontahss |
| playing cards | una baraja | oonah bahrahkhah |
| post cards | unas tarjetas postales | oonahss tahrkhaytahss poastahlayss |
| refill (for a pen) | un recambio (para pluma) | oon raykahmhyoa (pahrah ploomah) |
| rubber | una goma de borrar | oonah goamah day boarrahr |
| ruler | una regla | oonah rehglah |
| sketching block | un bloc de dibujo | oon bloak day deebookhoa |
| string | una cuerda | oonah kwayrdah |
| thumbtacks | chinchetas | choonchaytahss |
| tissue paper | papel de seda | pahpehl day saydhah |
| tracing paper | papel transparente | pahpehl trahnspahrayntay |
| typewriter ribbon | una cinta para máquina | oonah theentah pahrah mahkeenah |
| typing paper | papel de máquina | pahpehl day mahkeenah |
| wrapping paper | papel de envolver | pahpehl day aynbolbehr |
| writing pad | un bloc de papel | oon bloak day pahpehl |
| Where's the guide-book section? | ¿Dónde está la sección de libros-guía? | doanday aystah lah sayk-thyon day leebroass geeah |
| Where do you keep the English books? | ¿Dónde están los libros ingleses? | doanday aystahn loss leebroass eenglayssayss |

Here are some contemporary Spanish authors whose books are available in English translation:

| Rafael Alberti | Juan Goytisolo |
| Arrabal | Alvaro de Laiglesia |
| Francisco Candel | Antonio Machado |
| Federico García Lorca | José Luis Martín Vigil |
| José María Gironella | Jaime Salom |

## Camping

Here we're concerned with the equipment you may need.

| I'd like a/an/some... | Quisiera... | keessyayrah |
|---|---|---|
| axe | una hacha | oonah ahchah |
| bottle-opener | un abridor de botellas | oon ahbreedhor day boataylyahss |
| bucket | un cubo | oon koobhoa |
| butane gas | gas butano | gahss bootahnoa |
| camp-bed | una cama de campaña | oonah kahmah day kahmpahñah |
| camping equipment | un equipo de camping | oon aykeepoa day kahmpeeng |
| can opener | un abrelatas | oon ahbraylahtahss |
| candles | unas velas | oonahss baylahss |
| chair | una silla | oonah seelyah |
| folding chair | silla plegable | seelyah playgahblay |
| compass | una brújula | oonah brookhoolah |
| corkscrew | un sacacorchos | oon sahkahkoarchoass |
| crockery | una vajilla | oonah bahkheelyah |
| cutlery | una cubertería | oonah koobhehrtayreeah |
| deckchair | una silla de lona | oonah seelyah day loanah |
| first-aid kit | un botiquín | oon boateekeen |
| fishing tackle | un aparejo de pesca | oon ahpahrehkhoa day payskah |
| flashlight | una linterna | oonah leentehrnah |
| frying pan | una sartén | oonah sahrtayn |
| groundsheet | una alfombra (de hule) | oonah ahlfoambrah (day oolay) |
| hammer | un martillo | oon mahrteelyoa |
| hammock | una hamaca | oonah ahmahkah |
| ice-bag | un saco para hielo | oon sahkoa pahrah yayloa |
| kerosene | petróleo | paytroalehoa |
| kettle | una pava | oonah pahbhah |
| lamp | una lámpara | oonah lahmpahrah |
| lantern | un farolito | oon fahroaleetoa |
| matches | unas cerillas | oonahss thayreelyahss |
| mattress | un colchón | oon koalchon |
| methylated spirits | alcohol de quemar | ahlkaol day kaymahr |
| mosquito net | una red para mosquitos | oonah raydh pahrah moaskeetoass |
| paraffin | petróleo | paytroalehoa |
| penknife | un cortaplumas | oon koartahploomahss |
| picnic case | una bolsa para merienda | oonah boalsah pahrah mayryayndah |
| primus stove | un hornillo | oon oarneelyoa |

| rope | una cuerda | oonah kwayrdah |
| rucksack | una mochila | oonah moacheelah |
| saucepan | un cazo | oon kahthoa |
| screwdriver | un destornillador | oon daystoarneelyahdhor |
| scissors | unas tijeras | oonahss teekhayrahss |
| sheath knife | un cuchillo de estuche | oon koocheelyoa day ehstoochay |
| sleeping bag | un saco de dormir | oon sahkoa day doarmeer |
| stew pan | una cacerola | oonah kahthayroalah |
| stove | un infernillo | oon eenfehrneelyoa |
| table | una mesa | oonah mayssah |
| folding table | mesa plegable | mayssah playgahblay |
| tent | una tienda de campaña | oonah tyayndah day kahmpahñah |
| tent-peg | una estaca | oonah ehstahkah |
| tent-pole | un mástil | oon mahsteel |
| thermos flask (bottle) | un termo | oon tehrmoa |
| tin-opener | un abrelatas | oon ahbraylahtahss |
| tool kit | una caja de herramientas | oonah kahkhah day ehrrahmyayntahss |
| torch | una linterna | oonah leentehrnah |
| water carrier | una garrafa para agua | oonah gahrrahfah pahrah ahgwah |
| wood alcohol | alcohol de quemar | ahlkoaol day kaymahr |

## Crockery

| cups | unas tazas | oonahss tahthahss |
| food box | una flambrera | oonah fyahmbrayran |
| mugs | unas tazas altas sin plato | oonahss tahthahss ahltahss seen plahtoa |
| plates | unos platos | oonoass plahtoass |
| saucers | unos platos pequeños | oonoass plahtoass paykayñoass |

## Cutlery

| forks | unos tenedores | oonoass taynaydhoarayss |
| knives | unos cuchillos | oonoass koocheelyoass |
| spoons | unas cucharas | oonahss koochahrahss |
| teaspoons | unas cucharillas | oonahss koochahreelyahss |
| (made of) plastic | (de) plástico | (day) plahsteekoa |
| (made of) stainless steel | (de) acero inoxidable | (day) ahthayroa eenoakseedhahblay |

## Chemist's—Drugstore

A Spanish chemist's normally doesn't stock the great range of goods that you'll find in England or in the U.S. For example, he doesn't sell photographic equipment or books. And for perfume, make-up, etc., you must go to a *perfumería* (payrfoomay**ree**ah).

This section has been divided into two parts:

1. Pharmaceutical—medicine, first-aid, etc.
2. Toiletry—toilet articles, cosmetics

### General

| | | |
|---|---|---|
| Where's the nearest (all-night) chemist's? | ¿Dónde está la farmacia más cercana (de guardia)? | doanday aystah lah fahr-mahthyah mahss thehr-kahnah (day gwahrdyah) |
| What time does the chemist's open/close? | ¿A qué hora abren/cierran la farmacia? | ah kay oarah ahbrayn/thyerrahn lah fahrmahthyah |

### Part 1—Pharmaceutical

| | | |
|---|---|---|
| I want something for... | Quiero algo para... | kyayroa ahlgoa pahrah |
| a cold/a cough | un catarro/una tos | oon kahtahrroa/oonah toss |
| hay fever | la fiebre del heno | lah fyehbray dayl aynoa |
| a hangover | la resaca | lah rayssahkah |
| sunburn | las quemaduras del sol | lahss kaymahdhoorahss dayl sol |
| travel sickness | el mareo | ayl mahrehoa |
| an upset stomach | las molestias de estómago | lahss moalaystyahss day aystoamahgoa |
| Can you make up this prescription for me? | ¿Puede usted prepararme esta receta? | pwaydhay oostaydh pray-pahrahrmay aystah raythaytah |
| Shall I wait? | ¿Espero? | ayspayroa |
| When shall I come back? | ¿Cuándo vuelvo? | kwahndoa bwaylboa |
| Can I get it without a prescription? | ¿Puede dármelo sin receta? | pwaydhay dahrmayloa seen raythaytah |

FOR DOCTOR, see page 162

| Can I have a / an / some...? | ¿Puede darme...? | pwaydhay dahrmay |
|---|---|---|
| antiseptic cream | una crema anti-séptica | oonah kraymah ahntee-ssaypteekah |
| aspirins | unas aspirinas | oonahss ahspeereenahss |
| bandage | una venda | oonah bayndah |
| crepe bandage | venda de lienzo | bayndah day lyaynthoa |
| Band-Aids | esparadrapo | ehspahrahdrahpoa |
| calcium tablets | unas tabletas de calcio | oonahss tahblaytahss day kahlthyoa |
| contraceptives | unos anticoncep-tivos | oonoass ahnteekoanthayp-teebhoass |
| corn plasters | unas callicidas | oonahss kahlyeethee-dhahss |
| cotton wool | algodón | ahlgoadon |
| cough drops | unas gotas para la tos | oonahss goatahss pahrah lah toss |
| diabetic lozenges | unas pastillas para diabéticos | oonahss pahsteelyahss pahrah dyahbhayteekoass |
| disinfectant | desinfectante | daysseenfehktahntay |
| ear drops | gotas para los oídos | goatahss pahrah loss oaeedhoass |
| Elastoplast | esparadrapo | ehspahrahdrahpoa |
| eye drops | unas gotas para los ojos | oonahss goatahss pahrah loss okhoss |
| gargle | unos gargarismos | oonoass gahrgahreesmoass |
| gauze | gasa | gahssah |
| insect repellent | un repelente para insectos | oon raypaylayntay pahrah eensehktoass |
| iodine | yodo | yoadhoa |
| iron pills | unas píldoras de hierro | oonahss peeldoarahss day yehrroa |
| laxative | un laxante | oon lahksahntay |
| lint | unas hilas | oonahss eelahss |
| sanitary napkins | unas compresas | oonahss komprayssahss |
| sleeping pills | un somnífero | oon soamneefayroa |
| stomach pills | un digestivo | oon deekhaysteebhoa |
| surgical dressing | unas hilas | oonahss eelahss |
| throat lozenges | unas pastillas para la garganta | oonahss pasteelyahss pahrah lah gahrgahntah |
| tranquilizer | un sedante | oon saydhahntay |

| ¡VENENO! | POISON! |
|---|---|
| SOLO PARA USO EXTERNO | FOR EXTERNAL USE ONLY |

## Part 2—Toiletry

| I'd like a / an / some... | Quisiera... | keessyayrah |
|---|---|---|
| acne cream | una crema para el acné | oonah kraymah pahrah ayl ahknay |
| after-shave lotion | una loción para después del afeitado | oonah loathyon pahrah dayspwayss dayl ahfaytahdhoa |
| astringent | un astringente | oon ahstreenkhayntay |
| bath salts | sales de baño | sahlayss day bahñoa |
| cologne | agua de colonia | ahgwah day koaloanyah |
| cream | una crema | oonah kraymah |
| cleansing cream | limpiadora | leempyahdhoarah |
| cold cream | nutritiva | nootreeteebhah |
| foundation cream | maquillaje | mahkeelyahkhay |
| moisturizing cream | humedecedora | oomaydhaythaydhoarah |
| night cream | de noche | day noachay |
| cuticle remover | un quita-cutículas | oon keetah-kooteekoolahss |
| deodorant | un desodorante | oon dayssoadhoarahntay |
| emery boards | unas limas de papel | oonahss leemahss day pahpehl |
| eye liner | un perfilador de ojos | oon pehrfeelahdhor day okhoss |
| eye pencil | un lápiz de ojos | oon lahpeeth day okhoss |
| eye shadow | una sombra de ojos | oonah soambrah day okhoss |
| face powder | polvos de la cara | poalboass day lah kahrah |
| foot cream | una crema para los pies | oonah kraymah pahrah loss pyayss |
| hand cream / lotion | una crema / loción para las manos | oonah kraymah / loathyon pahrah lahss mahnoass |
| lipsalve | cacao para los labios | kahkahoa pahrah loss lahbhyoass |
| lipstick | un lápiz de labios | oon lahpeeth day lahbhyoass |
| make-up remover pads | unas toallitas de maquillage | oonahss toaahlyeetahss day mahkeelyahkhay |
| mascara | pintura de pestañas | peentoorah day pehstahñahss |
| nail clippers | alicates de uñas | ahleekahtayss day ooñahss |
| nail file | una lima de uñas | oonah leemah day ooñahss |
| nail polish | un esmalte de uñas | oon ehsmahltay day ooñahss |
| nail polish remover | acetona quita-esmalte de uñas | ahthaytoanah keetah ehsmahltay day ooñahss |
| nail scissors | tijeras de uñas | teekhayrahss day ooñahss |
| perfume | perfume | pehrfoomay |
| powder | polvos | poalboass |

| rouge | colorete | koaloaraytay |
| safety pins | unos imperdibles | oonoass eempehrdeeblayss |
| shampoo | champú | chahmpoo |
| shaving brush | una brocha de afeitar | oonah brochah day afaytahr |
| shaving cream | crema de afeitar | kraymah day afaytahr |
| shaving soap | jabón de afeitar | khahbon day afaytahr |
| soap | jabón | khahbon |
| sponge | una esponja | oonah ehsponkhah |
| sun-tan cream | una crema solar | oonah kraymah soalahr |
| sun-tan oil | un aceite solar | oon ahthaytay soalahr |
| talcum powder | polvos de talco | poalboass day tahlkoa |
| tissues | unos pañuelos de papel | oonoass pahñwayloass day pahpehl |
| toilet paper | papel higiénico | pahpehl eekhyayneekoa |
| toothbrush | un cepillo de dientes | oon thaypeelyoa day dyayntayss |
| toothpaste | pasta de dientes | pahstah day dyayntayss |
| tweezers | unas pinzas | oonahss peenthahss |

## For your hair

| bobby pins | unas horquillas | oonahss orkeelyahss |
| brush | un cepillo para el pelo | oon thaypeelyoa pahrah ayl pehloa |
| colouring | un tinte para el pelo | oon teentay pahrah ayl pehloa |
| comb | un peine | oon paynay |
| curlers | unos rulos | oonoass rooloass |
| dye | una tintura | oonah teentoorah |
| grips | unas horquillas de pinza | oonahss orkeelyahss day peenthah |
| oil | óleo para el pelo | olehoa pahrah ayl pehloa |
| pins | unos pinches | oonoass peenchayss |
| setting lotion | un fijador | oon feekhahdhor |
| spray | una laca para el pelo | oonah lahkah pahrah ayl pehloa |
| tint | un tinte | oon teentay |

## For the baby

| bib | un babero | oon bahbhayroa |
| dummy (pacifier) | un chupete | oon choopaytay |
| nappies (diapers) | pañales | pahñahlayss |
| nappy pins | imperdibles | eempehrdeeblayss |
| plastic pants | bragas de plástico | brahgahss day plahsteekoa |

## Clothing

If you want to buy something specific, prepare yourself in advance. Look at the list of clothing on page 117. Get some idea of the colour, material and size you want. They're all listed on the next few pages.

### General

| | | |
|---|---|---|
| I'd like... | **Quisiera...** | keessyayrah |
| I want...for a 10 year-old boy. | **Quiero...para un niño de 10 años.** | kyayroa...pahrah oon neeñoa day 10 ahñoass |
| I want something like this. | **Quiero algo como esto.** | kyayroa ahlgoa koamoa aystoa |
| I like the one in the window. | **Me gusta el que está en el escaparate.** | may goostah ayl kay aystah ayn ayl eskahpah-rahtay |
| How much is that per metre? | **¿Cuánto cuesta el metro?** | kwahntoa kwaystah ayl mehtroa |

| | | | |
|---|---|---|---|
| 1 centimetre = | 0.39 in. | 1 inch = | 2.54 cm. |
| 1 metre | = 39.37 in. | 1 foot = | 30.5 cm. |
| 10 metres | = 32.81 ft. | 1 yard = | 0.91 m. |

### Colour

| | | |
|---|---|---|
| I want something in... | **Quiero algo en...** | kyayroa ahlgoa ayn |
| I want a darker shade. | **Quiero un tono más oscuro.** | kyayroa oon toanoa mahss oaskooroa |
| I want something to match this. | **Quiero algo que haga juego con esto.** | kyayroa ahlgoa kay ahgah khwaygoa kon aystoa |
| I don't like the colour. | **No me gusta el color.** | noa may goostah ayl koalor |

**rayas**
(rahyahss)

**lunares**
(loonahrayss)

**cuadros**
(kwahdroass)

**estampado**
(ehstahmpahdhoa)

| beige | **beige** | "behzh" |
| black | **negro** | nehgroa |
| blue | **azul** | ahthool |
| brown | **marrón** | mahrron |
| cream | **crema** | kraymah |
| crimson | **carmesí** | kahrmayssee |
| emerald | **verde esmeralda** | behrday aysmayrahldah |
| fawn | **marrón claro** | mahrron klahroa |
| golden | **oro** | oaroa |
| green | **verde** | behrday |
| grey | **gris** | greess |
| mauve | **malva** | mahlbah |
| orange | **naranja** | nahrahnkhah |
| pink | **rosa** | rossah |
| purple | **purpúreo** | poorpoorehoa |
| red | **rojo** | roakhoa |
| scarlet | **escarlata** | ayskahrlahtah |
| silver | **plata** | plahtah |
| turquoise | **turquesa** | toorkayssah |
| white | **blanco** | blahnkoa |
| yellow | **amarillo** | ahmahreelyoa |

## Material

| Do you have anything in...? | **¿Tiene usted algo en...?** | tyaynay oostaydh ahlgoa ayn |
| I want a cotton blouse. | **Quisiera una blusa de algodón.** | keessyayrah oonah bloo-sah day ahlgoadon |
| Is that imported? | **¿Es eso importado?** | ayss ayssoa eempor-tahdhoa |
| Is that...? | **¿Está hecho...?** | aystah aychoa |
| hand-made / made here | **a mano / aquí** | ah mahnoa / ahkee |
| I want something thinner. | **Quiero algo más tenue.** | kyayroa ahlgoa mahss taynooay |
| Do you have any better quality? | **¿Tiene usted una calidad mejor?** | tyaynay oostaydh oonah kahleedhahdh mehkhor |
| What's it made of? | **¿De qué está hecho?** | day kay aystah aychoa |

It may be made of…

| cambric | batista | bahteestah |
| camel hair | pelo de camello | pehloa day kahmaylyoa |
| chiffon | gasa | gahssah |
| corduroy | pana | pahnah |
| cotton | algodón | ahlgoadon |
| crepe | crepé | kraypay |
| denim | algodón asargado | ahlgoadon ahssahrgahdhoa |
| felt | fieltro | fyayltroa |
| flannel | franela | frahnaylah |
| gabardine | gabardina | gahbhahrdeenah |
| lace | encaje | aynkahkhay |
| leather | cuero | kwayroa |
| linen | hilo | eeloa |
| pique | piqué | peekay |
| poplin | popelín | poapayleen |
| rayon | rayón | rehyon |
| satin | raso | rahssoa |
| serge | estameña | aystahmayñah |
| silk | seda | saydhah |
| suede | ante | ahntay |
| taffeta | tafetán | tahfaytahn |
| terrycloth | tela de toalla | taylah day toaahlyah |
| tulle | tul | tool |
| tweed | cheviot | chaybhyoat |
| velvet | terciopelo | tehrthyoapehloa |
| wool | lana | lahnah |
| worsted | estambre | aystahmbray |
| | | |
| artificial | artificial | ahrteefeethyahl |
| synthetic | sintético | seentayteekoa |
| wash and wear | no se necesita planchar | noa say naythaysseetah plahnchahr |
| wrinkle-resistant | inarrugable | eenahrroogahblay |

## Size

| My size is 38. | Mi talla es la 38. | mee tahlyah ayss lah 38 |
| Could you measure me? | ¿Puede usted medirme? | pwaydhay oostaydh maydheermay |
| I don't know the Spanish sizes. | No conozco las tallas españolas. | noa koanoathkoa lahss tahlyahss ayspahñolahss |

In that case, look at the charts on the next page.

## This is your size

In Europe sizes vary somewhat from country to country, so this table must be taken as an approximate guide.

### Ladies

| Dresses/Suits | | | | | |
|---|---|---|---|---|---|
| American | 10 | 12 | 14 | 15 | 18 | 20 |
| British | 32 | 34 | 36 | 38 | 40 | 42 |
| Continental | 38 | 40 | 42 | 44 | 46 | 48 |

| Stockings | | | | | | | Shoes | | | |
|---|---|---|---|---|---|---|---|---|---|
| American )  British } | 8 | 8½ | 9 | 9½ | 10 | 10½ | 6  4½ | 7  5½ | 8  6½ | 9  7½ |
| Continental | 0 | 1 | 2 | 3 | 4 | 5 | 37 | 39 | 40 | 41 |

### Gentlemen

| Suits/Overcoats | | | | | | Shirts | | | |
|---|---|---|---|---|---|---|---|---|---|
| American  British | 36 | 38 | 40 | 42 | 44 | 46 | 15 | 16 | 17 | 18 |
| Continental | 46 | 48 | 50 | 52 | 54 | 56 | 38 | 41 | 43 | 45 |

| Shoes | | | | | | | | | |
|---|---|---|---|---|---|---|---|---|---|
| American  British | 5 | 6 | 7 | 8 | 8½ | 9 | 9½ | 10 | 11 |
| Continental | 38 | 39 | 41 | 42 | 43 | 43 | 44 | 44 | 45 |

## A good fit ?

| Can I try it on ? | ¿Puedo probár-melo ? | pwaydhoa probhahr-mayloa |
|---|---|---|
| Where's the fitting room ? | ¿Dónde está el probador ? | doanday aystah ayl probhahdhor |
| Is there a mirror ? | ¿Tiene usted un espejo ? | tyaynay oostaydh oon ayspehkhoa |
| Does it fit ? | ¿Me queda bien ? | may kaydhah byayn |
| It fits very well. | Me está muy bien. | may aystah mwee byayn |

FOR NUMBERS, see page 175

SHOPPING GUIDE

| It doesn't fit. | **No me está bien.** | noa may ay**stah** byayn |
| It's too... | **Es demasiado...** | ayss daymah**ssyah**dhoa |
| short / long | **corto / largo** | **koar**toa / **lahr**goa |
| tight / loose | **apretado / suelto** | ahpray**tah**dhoa / **sway**ltoa |
| How long will it take to alter? | **¿Cuánto tardarán en arreglarlo?** | **kwahn**toa tahrdah**rahn** ayn ahrray**glahr**loa |

## Shoes

| I'd like a pair of... | **Quisiera un par de...** | kee**ssyay**rah oon pahr day |
| shoes / sandals | **zapatos / sandalias** | thah**pah**toass / sanh**dah**lyahss |
| boots / slippers | **botas / zapatillas** | **boa**tahss / thapah**tee**lyahss |
| These are too... | **Estas son demasiado...** | **ays**tahss son daymah**ssyah**dhoa |
| narrow / wide | **estrechas / amplias** | ays**tray**chahss / **ahm**pleeahss |
| large / small | **grandes / pequeñas** | **grahn**dayss / pay**kay**ñahss |
| They pinch my toes. | **Me hacen daño en los dedos.** | may **ah**thayn **dah**ñoa ayn los **dehd**hoass |
| Do you have a larger size? | **¿Tiene una talla más grande?** | **tyay**nay oonah **tah**lyah mahss **grahn**day |
| I want a smaller size. | **Quiero una talla más pequeña.** | **kyay**roa oonah **tah**lyah mahss pay**kay**ñah |
| Do you have the same in...? | **¿Tiene usted lo mismo en...?** | **tyay**nay oos**taydh** loa **mees**moa ayn |
| brown / beige | **marrón / beige** | mah**rron** / **behz** |
| black / white | **negro / blanco** | **neh**groa / **blahn**koa |

Shoes worn out? Here's the key to getting them fixed again:

| Can you repair these shoes? | **¿Puede usted reparar estos zapatos?** | **pway**dhay oos**taydh** rehpah**rahr** **ays**toass thah**pah**toass |
| Can you stitch this? | **¿Puede coser esto?** | **pway**dhay koa**ssehr** **ays**toa |
| I want new soles and heels. | **Quiero nuevas suelas y tacones.** | **kyay**roa **nway**bhahss **sway**lahss ee tah**koa**nayss |
| When will they be ready? | **¿Cuándo estarán listos?** | **kwahn**doa aysta**rahn** **lees**toass |

## Clothes and accessories

| I'd like a / an / some... | Quisiera... | keessyayrah |
|---|---|---|
| bathing cap | un gorro de baño | oon gorroa day bahñoa |
| bathing suit | un traje de baño | oon trahkhay day bahñoa |
| bath robe | un albornoz | oon ahlboarnoth |
| blazer | un blazer | oon blahther |
| blouse | una blusa | oonah bloossah |
| bow tie | una corbata de lazo | oonah korbahtah day lahthoa |
| bra | un sostén | oon soastayn |
| braces | unos tirantes | oonoass teerahntayss |
| briefs | unos calzoncillos | oonoass kahlthontheelyoass |
| cap | una gorra | oonah gorrah |
| cardigan | una chaqueta de punto | oonah chakaytah day poontoa |
| coat (woman's) | un abrigo | oon ahbreegoa |
| coat (man's) | un gabán | oon gahbhahn |
| dinner jacket | un smoking | oon smoakeeng |
| dress | un vestido | oon baysteedhoa |
| dressing gown | una bata | oonah bahtah |
| evening dress | un traje de noche | oon trahkhay day noachay |
| frock | un vestido | oon baysteedhoa |
| garter belt | un portaligas | oon poartahleegahss |
| garters | unas ligas | oonahss leegahss |
| girdle | una faja | oonah fahkhah |
| gloves | unos guantes | oonoass gwahntayss |
| gym shoes | unos zapatos de gimnasia | oonoass thapahtoass day kheemnahssyah |
| handkerchief | un pañuelo | oon pahñwayloa |
| hat | un sombrero | oon soambrayroa |
| jacket | una chaqueta | oonah chachkaytah |
| jeans | unos tejanos | oonoass tehkhahnoass |
| negligé | un negligé | oon "négligé" |
| nightdress | un camisón | oon kahmeesson |
| overalls | unos guardapolvos | oonoass gwahrdahpoalboass |
| panties | unas bragas | oonahss brahgahss |
| pants suit | un traje-pantalón | oon trahkhay pahntahlon |
| panty-girdle | una faja braga | oonah fahkhah brahgah |
| panty hose | unos "panties" | oonoass pahnteess |
| pullover | un "pullover" | oon pooloabhehr |
| pyjamas | un pijama | oon peekhahmah |
| raincoat | un impermeable | oon eempehrmayahblay |
| sandals | unas sandalias | oonahss sahndahlyahss |
| scarf | una bufanda | oonah boofahndah |

| | | |
|---|---|---|
| shirt | **una camisa** | oonah kah**mee**ssah |
| shoes | **unos zapatos** | oonoass thah**pah**toass |
| shorts | **unos pantalones cortos** | oonoass pahntah**loa**nayss **koar**toass |
| skirt | **una falda** | oonah **fahl**dah |
| slip | **una combinación de medio cuerpo** | oonah koambeenah**thyon** day **meh**dhyoa **kwehr**poa |
| slippers | **unas zapatillas** | oonahss thahpah**tee**lyahss |
| socks | **unos calcetines** | oonoass kahlthay**tee**nayss |
| stockings | **unas medias** | oonahss **meh**dhyahss |
| stole | **una estola** | oonah eh**stoa**lah |
| suit (man's) | **un traje** | oon **trah**khay |
| suit (woman's) | **un vestido** | oon bay**stee**dhoa |
| suspender belt | **un liguero** | oon lee**gay**roa |
| suspenders | **unos tirantes** | oonoass tee**rahn**tayss |
| sweater | **un suéter** | oon **sway**tehr |
| sweatshirt | **un suéter de tela de punto** | oon **sway**tehr day **tay**lah day **poon**toa |
| T-shirt | **una camiseta** | oonah kahmee**ssay**tah |
| tennis shoes | **unos zapatos de tenis** | oonoass thah**pah**toass day **teh**nees |
| tie | **una corbata** | oonah kor**bah**tah |
| tights | **unos leotardos** | oonoass layoa**tahr**doass |
| track suit | **un chandal de entrenamiento** | oon chahn**dahl** day ehntraynah**myay**ntoa |
| trousers | **unos pantalones** | oonoass pahntah**loa**nayss |
| tuxedo | **un smoking** | oon **smoa**keeng |
| twin set | **un conjunto de lana** | oon koan**khoon**toa day **lah**nah |
| underpants (men) | **unos calzoncillos** | oonoass kahlthon**thee**lyoass |
| undershirt | **una camiseta** | oonah kahmee**ssay**tah |
| vest (Am.) | **un chaleco** | oon chah**lay**koa |
| vest (Br.) | **una camiseta** | oonah kahmee**ssay**tah |
| waistcoat | **un chaleco** | oon chah**lay**koa |

| | | |
|---|---|---|
| belt | **un cinturón** | oon theentoo**ron** |
| buckle | **una hebilla** | oonah ay**bhee**lyah |
| button | **un botón** | oon bo**ton** |
| cuffs | **unos gemelos** | oonoass khay**may**loass |
| elastic | **un elástico** | oon ay**lahs**teekoa |
| pocket | **un bolsillo** | oon bol**see**lyoa |
| shoe laces | **unos cordones de zapatos** | oonoass kor**do**nayss day thah**pah**toass |
| zip (zipper) | **una cremallera** | oonah kraymahl**lay**rah |

## Electrical appliances and accessories—Records

In most hotels and boarding houses the voltage is 110–125 volts, 50-cycle AC. However, 220–230 volts is also used. So check the voltage before you plug your appliance in.

You may also find an adaptor plug useful as some continental plugs are different from ours.

| | | |
|---|---|---|
| What's the voltage? | ¿Cuál es el voltaje? | kwahl ayss ayl boaltahkhay |
| I want a plug for this. | Quisiera un enchufe para esto. | keessyayrah oon aynchoo-fay pahrah aystoa |
| Do you have a battery for this? | ¿Tiene usted una pila para esto? | tyaynay oostaydh oonah peelah pahrah aystoa |
| This is broken. Can you repair it? | Esto está roto. ¿Puede usted arreglarlo? | aystoa aystah roatoa. pwaydhay oostaydh ahrrayglahrloa |
| When will it be ready? | ¿Cuándo estará listo? | kwahndoa aystahrah leestoa |
| I'd like a / an / some... | Quisiera... | keessyayrah |
| adaptor | un adaptador | oon ahdahptahdhor |
| amplifier | un amplificador | oon ahmpleefeekahdhor |
| battery | una pila | oonah peelah |
| blender | una batidora | oonah bahteedhoarah |
| clock | un reloj | oon rehlokh |
|   wall clock | un reloj de pared | oon rehlokh day pahraydh |
| food mixer | una batidora | oonah bahteedhoarah |
| hair dryer | un secador de pelo | oon saykahdhor day pehloa |
| iron | una plancha | oonah plahnchah |
|   travelling-iron | una plancha de viaje | oonah plahnchah day byahkhay |
| kettle | una pava | oonah pahbhah |
| percolator | una cafetera | oonah kahfaytayrah |
| plug | un enchufe | oon aynchoofay |
| portable... | ...portátil | ...portahteel |
| radio | una radio | oonah rahdhyoa |
|   car radio | una radio para automóvil | oonah rahdhyoa pahrah owtoamoabheel |
| record player | un tocadiscos | oon toakahdheeskoass |
| shaver | una máquina de afeitar eléctrica | oonah mahkeenah day ahfaytahr aylayktreekah |
| speakers | unos altavoces | oonoass ahltahbhoathayss |

| tape recorder | **un magnetófono** | oon mahgnaytofoanoa |
| cassette tape recorder | **un magnetófono "cassette"** | oon mahgnaytofoanoa "kahssayt" |
| television | **un televisor** | oon taylaybheessor |
| colour television | **un televisor en color** | oon taylaybheessor ayn koalor |
| toaster | **una tostadora** | oonah toastahdhoarah |
| transformer | **un transformador** | oon trahnsformahdhor |

## Music

| Do you have any records by... ? | **¿Tiene usted algún disco de... ?** | tyaynay oostaydh ahlgoon deeskoa day |
| Do you have...'s latest album ? | **¿Tiene usted el último álbum de... ?** | tyaynay oostaydh ayl oolteemoa ahlboom day |
| I'd like a cassette. | **Quisiera un caseta para magnetófono.** | keessyayrah oon kahssaytah pahrah mahgnaytofoanoa |
| I want a new needle. | **Quiero una aguja nueva.** | kyayroa oonah ahgookhah nwaybhah |

| L.P. | **un "Long-Play"** | oon "long-play" |
| 33 rpm | **un disco 33** | oon deeskoa trayntah ee trayss |
| 45 rpm | **un disco 45** | oon deeskoa kwahrayntah ee theenkoa |

| chamber music | **música de cámara** | moosseekah day kahmahrah |
| classical music | **música clásica** | moosseekah klahsseekah |
| folk music | **música folklórica** | moosseekah folkloareekah |
| instrumental music | **música instrumental** | moosseekah eenstroomayntahl |
| jazz | **jazz** | "jazz" |
| light music | **música ligera** | moosseekah leekhayrah |
| orchestral music | **música de orquesta** | moosseekah day orkaystrah |
| pop music | **música pop** | moosseekah pop |

Here are the names of a few popular recording artists:

| | |
| --- | --- |
| Conchita Bautista | Conchita Piquer |
| Manolo Escobar | Raphael |
| Paco Ibañez | Miguel Ríos |
| Julio Iglesias | Joan-Manuel Serrat |
| Marisol | Mari Trini |
| Antonio Molina | Juanito Valderrama |

## Hairdressing—At the barber's

| | | |
|---|---|---|
| I don't speak much Spanish. | **No hablo mucho español.** | noa ahbloa moochoa ayspahñol |
| I'm in a hurry. | **Tengo prisa.** | tayngoa preessah |
| I want a haircut, please. | **Quiero un corte de pelo, por favor.** | kyayroa oon kortay day pehloa por fahbhor |
| I'd like a shave. | **Quisiera que me afeitaran.** | keessyayrah kay may ahfaytahrahn |
| Don't cut it too short. | **No me lo corte mucho.** | noa may loa koartay moochoa |
| Scissors only, please. | **Sólo con tijeras, por favor.** | soaloa kon teekhayrahss por fahbhor |
| A razor cut, please. | **A navaja, por favor.** | ah nahbhahkhah por fahbhor |
| Don't use the clippers. | **No use las tijeras.** | noa oossay lahss teekhayrahss |
| Just a trim, please. | **Sólo recórtemelo un poco, por favor.** | soaloa rehkortaymayloa oon poakoa por fahbhor |
| That's enough off. | **Eso es bastante.** | ayssoa ayss bahstahntay |
| A little more off the... | **Un poco más...** | oon poakoa mahss |
| back | **por detrás** | por daytrahss |
| neck | **en el cuello** | ayn ayl kwaylyoa |
| sides | **en los lados** | ayn loss lahdhoass |
| top | **arriba** | anrreebhah |
| Please don't use any oil. | **Por favor, no me dé ningún aceite.** | por fahbhor noa may day neengoon ahthaytay |
| Would you please trim my...? | **¿Quiere usted recortarme...?** | kyayray oostaydh rehkortahrmay |
| beard | **la barba** | lah bahrbah |
| moustache | **el bigote** | ayl beegoatay |
| sideboards (sideburns) | **las patillas** | lahss pahteelyahss |
| Thank you. That's fine. | **Gracias. Está muy bien.** | grahthyahss. aystah mwee byayn |
| How much do I owe you? | **¿Cuánto le debo?** | kwahntoa lay daybhoa |
| This is for you. | **Esto es para usted.** | aystoa ayss pahrah oostaydh |

## Ladies' hairdressing

| | | |
|---|---|---|
| Is there a hairdresser's in the hotel? | ¿Hay una peluquería en el hotel? | igh oonah paylookayreeah ayn ayl oatehl |
| Can I make an appointment for some-time on Thursday? | ¿Puedo pedir hora para el jueves? | pwaydhoa pehdheer oarah pahrah ayl khwaybhayss |
| I'd like it cut and shaped. | Quiero que me lo corten y le den forma. | kyayroa kay may loa kortayn ee lay dayn formah |

| with a fringe (bangs) | con flequillo | kon flaykeelyoa |
|---|---|---|
| page-boy style | a lo paje | ah loa pahkhay |
| a razor cut | cortado a navaja | kortahdhoa ah nahbhahkhah |
| a re-style | volver a dar forma | bolbehr ah dahr formah |
| with ringlets | con rizos | kon reethoass |
| with waves | con ondas | kon oandahss |
| in a bun | con un moño | kon oon moañoa |

| | | |
|---|---|---|
| I want a... | Quiero... | kyayroa |
| bleach | aclarármelo | ahklahrahrmayloa |
| colour rinse | un reflejo | oon rehflaykhoa |
| dye | teñírmelo | tayñeermayloa |
| permanent | una permanente | oonah pehrmahnayntay |
| shampoo and set | lavado y marcado | lahbhahdhoa ee mahrkahdhoa |
| tint | un tinte | oon teentay |
| touch up | un retoque | oon raytoakay |
| the same colour | el mismo color | ayl meesmoa koalor |
| a darker colour | un color más oscuro | oon koalor mahss oskooroa |
| a lighter colour | un color más claro | oon koalor mahss klahroa |
| auburn / blond / brunette | rojizo / rubio / castaño | roakheethoa / roobyoa / kahstahñoa |
| Do you have a colour chart? | ¿Tiene usted un muestrario? | tyaynay oostaydh oon mwaystrahryoa |
| I don't want any hairspray. | No quiero laca. | noa kyayroa lahkah |
| I want a... | Quiero... | kyayroa |
| manicure | una manicura | oonah mahneekoorah |
| pedicure | una pedicura | oonah paydheekoorah |
| face-pack | una máscara de belleza | oonah mahsskahrah day baylyaythah |

## Jeweller's—Watchmaker's

| | | |
|---|---|---|
| Can you repair this watch? | ¿Puede arreglar este reloj? | pwaydhay ahrrayglahr aystay rehlokh |
| The...is broken. | ...está roto/rota. | ...aystah roatoa/roatah |
| glass/spring | el cristal/el resorte | ayl kreestahl/ayl rayssortay |
| strap/winder | la correa/la cuerda | lah korrehah/lah kwayrdah |
| I want this watch cleaned. | Quiero que me limpien este reloj. | kyayroa kay may leempyayn aystay rehlokh |
| When will it be ready? | ¿Cuándo estará listo? | kwahndoa aystahrah leestoa |
| Could I please see that? | ¿Puedo ver eso, por favor? | pwaydhoa behr ayssoa por fahbhor |
| I'm just looking around. | Sólo estoy mirando. | soaloa aystoy meerahndoa |
| I want a small present for... | Quiero un regalito para... | kyayroa oon raygahleetoa pahrah |
| I don't want anything too expensive. | No quiero nada demasiado caro. | noa kyayroa nahdhah daymahsseeyahdhoa kahroa |
| I want something... | Quiero algo... | kyayroa ahlgoa |
| better/cheaper simpler | mejor/más barato más sencillo | mehkhor/mahss bahrahtoa mahss sayntheeiyoa |
| Is this real silver? | ¿Es esto de plata auténtica? | ayss aystoa day plahtah owtaynteekah |
| Do you have anything in gold? | ¿Tiene usted algo de oro? | tyaynay oostaydh ahlgoa day oaroa |

If it's made of gold, ask:

| | | |
|---|---|---|
| How many carats is this? | ¿De cuántos quilates es esto? | day kwahntoass keelahtayss ayss aystoa |

When you go to a jeweller's, you've probably got some idea of what you want beforehand. Find out what the article is made of, and then look up the name of the article itself in the following lists.

SHOPPING GUIDE

## What's it made of ?

| | | |
|---|---|---|
| amber | **ámbar** | ahmbahr |
| amethyst | **amatista** | ahmahteestah |
| chromium | **cromo** | kromoa |
| copper | **cobre** | koabray |
| coral | **coral** | korahl |
| crystal | **cristal** | kreestahl |
| cut glass | **cristal tallado** | kreestahl tahlyahdhoa |
| diamond | **diamante** | dyahmahntay |
| ebony | **ébano** | ehbbahnoa |
| emerald | **esmeralda** | aysmayrahldah |
| enamel | **esmaltado** | aysmahltahdhoa |
| glass | **cristal** | kreestahl |
| gold | **oro** | oaroa |
| gold plated | **lámina de oro** | lahmeenah day oaroa |
| ivory | **marfil** | mahrfeel |
| jade | **jade** | khahdheh |
| onyx | **ónix** | oneekss |
| pearl | **perla** | pehrlah |
| pewter | **peltre** | pehltray |
| platinum | **platino** | plahteenoa |
| ruby | **rubí** | roobhee |
| sapphire | **zafiro** | thahfeeroa |
| silver | **plata** | plahtah |
| silver plated | **plata chapada** | plahtah chahpahdhah |
| stainless steel | **acero inoxidable** | ahthehroa eenokseedhah-blay |
| topaz | **topacio** | topahthyoa |
| turquoise | **turquesa** | toorkayssah |

## What is it ?

| | | |
|---|---|---|
| I'd like a / an / some... | **Quisiera...** | keessyayrah |
| bangle | **una esclava** | oonah aysklahbhah |
| beads | **un collar de cuentas** | oon koalyahr day kwayntahss |
| bracelet | **una pulsera** | oonah poolsayrah |
| charm bracelet | **pulsera de fetiches** | poolsayrah day fayteechayss |
| brooch | **un broche** | oon brochay |
| chain | **una cadena** | oonah kahdhaynah |
| charm | **un amuleto** | oon ahmoolehtoa |
| cigarette case | **una pitillera** | oonah peeteelyayrah |
| cigarette lighter | **un encendedor** | oon aynthayndhaydhor |
| clip | **un clip** | oon kleep |

| | | |
|---|---|---|
| clock | un reloj | oon rehlokh |
| alarm clock | un despertador | oon dayspayrtahdhor |
| travelling clock | un despertador de viaje | oon dayspayrtahdhor day byahkhay |
| collar stud | un cierre de collar | oon thyehrray day koalyahr |
| cross | una cruz | oonah krooth |
| cuff-links | unos gemelos | oonoass khaymayloass |
| cutlery | unos cubiertos | oonoass koobhyehrtoass |
| earrings | unos pendientes | oonoass payndyayntayss |
| jewel box | un joyero | oon khoyehroa |
| manicure set | un estuche de manicura | oon aystoochay day mahneekoorah |
| mechanical pencil | un lapicero | oon lahpeethayroa |
| necklace | un collar | oon koalyahr |
| pendant | un medallón | oon maydhahlyon |
| pin | un alfiler | oon ahlfeelehr |
| powder compact | una polvera | oonah poalbehrah |
| propelling pencil | un lapicero | oon lahpeethayroa |
| ring | una sortija | oonah sorteekhah |
| engagement ring | sortija de pedida | sorteekhah day paydheedhah |
| signet ring | sortija de sello | sorteekhah day saylyoa |
| wedding ring | un anillo de boda | oon ahneelyoa day boadhah |
| rosary | un rosario de cuentas | oon roassahryoa day kwayntahss |
| silverware | unos objetos de plata | oonoass obkhehtoass day plahtah |
| snuff box | una cajita de rapé | oonah kahkheetah day rahpay |
| strap | una correa | oonah korrehah |
| chain strap | correa en forma de cadena | korrehah ayn foarmah day kahdhaynah |
| leather strap | correa de cuero | korrehah day kwayroa |
| watch strap | correa de reloj | korrehah day rehlokh |
| tie clip | un sujetador de corbata | oon sookhaytahdhor day korbahtah |
| tie pin | un alfiler de corbata | oon ahlfeelehr day korbahtah |
| vanity case | un neceser | oon naythayssehr |
| watch | un reloj | oon rehlokh |
| pocket watch | reloj de bolsillo | rehlokh day boalseelyoa |
| with a second hand | con segundero manecilla | kon saygoondayroa mah-naytheelyah |
| wristwatch | reloj de pulsera | rehlokh day poolsayrah |

### Laundry—Dry cleaning

If your hotel doesn't have its own laundry or dry cleaning service, ask the porter:

| | | |
|---|---|---|
| Where's the nearest laundry / dry cleaner's? | ¿Dónde está la lavandería/tintorería más cercana? | doanday aystah lah lah-bhahndayreeah/teentoarayreeah mahss thehrkahnah |
| I want these clothes... | Quiero que...esta ropa. | kyayroa kay...aystah roapah |
| cleaned | limpien | leempyayn |
| ironed / pressed | planchen | plahnchayn |
| washed | laven | lahbhayn |
| When will it be ready? | ¿Cuándo estará lista? | kwahndoa aystahrah leestah |
| I need it... | La necesito para... | lah naythaysseetoa pahrah |
| today | hoy | oy |
| tonight | esta noche | aystah noachay |
| tomorrow | mañana | mahñahnah |
| before Friday | antes del viernes | ahntayss dayl byehrnayss |
| Can you...this? | ¿Puede usted...esto? | pwaydhay oostaydh...aystoa |
| mend | remendar | rehmayndahr |
| patch | poner un parche | poanehr oon pahrchay |
| stitch | hilvanar | eelbahnahr |
| Can you sew on this button? | ¿Puede usted coser este botón? | pwaydhay oostaydh koassehr aystay boaton |
| Can you get this stain out? | ¿Puede usted quitar esta mancha? | pwaydhay oostaydh keetahr aystah mahnchah |
| Can this be invisibly mended? | ¿Puede usted hacer un zurcido invisible? | pwaydhay oostaydh ahthehr oon thoortheedhoa eenbeesseeblay |
| This isn't mine. | Esto no es mío. | aystoa noa ayss meeoa |
| There's one piece missing. | Falta una prenda. | fahltah oonah prayndah |
| There's a hole in this. | Hay un hoyo aquí. | igh oon oayoa ahkee |
| Is my laundry ready? | ¿Está ya mi ropa lavada? | aystah yah mee roapah lahbhahdhah |

## Photography

| I want an inexpensive camera. | Quiero una cámara barata. | kyayroa oonah kahmahrah bahrahtah |
| Show me the one in the window. | Enséñeme la del escaparate. | aynsayñaymay lah dayl ayskahpahrahtay |

## Film

Film sizes aren't always indicated the same way in Europe as in the United States and Great Britain. Listed below you'll find some translations that will be useful.

| I'd like a... | Quisiera... | keessyayrah |
| cartridge | un rollo | oon roalyoa |
| film for this camera | una película para esta cámara | oonah payleekoolah pahrah aystah kahmahrah |
| a... film | una película... | oonah payleekoolah |
| 120 | ciento veinte | thyayntoa bayntay |
| 126 | ciento veintiséis | thyayntoa baynteessayss |
| 135 | ciento treinta y cinco | thyayntoa trayntah ee theenkoa |
| 620 (roll film) | seiscientos veinte (rollo) | saysthyayntoass bayntay (roalyoa) |
| 8 mm | ocho milímetros | oachoa meeleemohtroass |
| super 8 | super ocho | soopehr oachoa |
| 16-mm | dieciséis milímetros | dyaytheessayss meeleemeht-troass |
| 20 exposures | veinte exposiciones | bayntay aykspoassee-thyonayss |
| 36 exposures | treinta y seis exposiciones | trayntah ee sayss aykspoasseethyonayss |
| this ASA/DIN number | este número de ASA/DIN | aystay noomayroa day ahssah/deen |
| fast | rápido | rahpeedhoa |
| fine grain | de grano fino | day grahnoa feenoa |
| black and white | en blanco y negro | ayn blahnkoa ee naygroa |
| colour | en color | ayn koalor |
| colour negative | negativo de color | naygahteebhoa day koalor |
| colour slide | diapositivo | dyahpoasseeteebhoa |
| artificial light type | para luz artificial | pahrah looth ahrteefee-thyahl |
| daylight type | para luz del día | pahrah looth dayl deeah |

FOR NUMBERS, see page 175

SHOPPING GUIDE

### Processing

| | | |
|---|---|---|
| How much do you charge for developing/printing? | ¿Qué cobra por el revelado/la impresión? | kay koabrah por ayl raybhaylahdhoa/lah eemprayssyon |
| I want...prints of each negative. | Quiero...copias de cada negativo. | kyayroa ... koapyahss day kahdah naygateebhoa |
| with a glossy finish | con acabado de brillo | kon ahkahbhahdhoa day breelyoa |
| with a mat finish | con acabado mate | kon ahkahbhahdhoa mahtay |
| Will you please enlarge this? | ¿Haría usted una ampliación de ésta, por favor? | ahreeah oostayhd oonah ahmplyahthyon day aystah por fahbhor |

### Accessories

| | | |
|---|---|---|
| I want a/an/some... | Quisiera... | keessyayrah |
| filter | un filtro | oon feeltroa |
| red/yellow | rojo/amarillo | roakhoa/ahmahreelyoa |
| ultraviolet | ultravioleta | ooltrahbhyoalaytah |
| flash bulbs/cubes | unas bombillas/ unos cubitos de flash | oonahss boambeelyahss/ oonoass koobheetoass day flash |
| for black and white | para blanco y negro | pahrah blahnkoa ee naygroa |
| for colour | para color | pahrah koalor |
| lens cap | un capuchón para el objetivo | oon kahpoochon pahrah ayl obkhayteebhoa |

### Broken

| | | |
|---|---|---|
| This camera doesn't work. Can you repair it? | Esta cámara está estropeada. ¿Puede usted repararla? | aystah kahmahrah aystah aystroapehahdhah. pwaydha oostaydh raypahrahrlah |
| The film is jammed. | La película está atrancada. | lah payleekoolah aystah ahtrahnkahdhah |
| There's something wrong with the... | Hay algo que va mal en... | igh ahlgoa kay bah mahl ayn |
| exposure counter | la escala de exposición | lah ayskahlah day aykspoasseethyon |
| film winder | el enrollador | ayl aynroalyahdhor |
| lightmeter | el exposímetro | ayl aykspoasseemehtroa |
| shutter | el obturador | ayl obtoorahdhor |

## Provisions

Here's a basic list of food and drink that you might want on a picnic or for the occasional meal at home:

| I'd like a / some... | Quisiera... | keessyayrah |
|---|---|---|
| apples | manzanas | mahnthahnahss |
| bananas | unos plátanos | oonoass plahtahnoass |
| biscuits (Br.) | unas galletas | oonahss gahlyaytahss |
| bread | pan | pahn |
| butter | mantequilla | mahntaykeelyah |
| cake | unos bollos / pasteles | oonoass boalyoass / pahstaylayss |
| candy | unos caramelos | oonoass kahrahmayloass |
| cheese | queso | kehssoa |
| chocolate | chocolate | choakoalahtay |
| coffee | café | kahfay |
| cold cuts | unos fiambres | oonoass fyahmbrayss |
| cookies | unas galletas | oonahss gahlyaytahss |
| cooking fat | grasa para cocinar | grahssah pahrah koatheenahr |
| crackers | unas galletas saladas | oonahss gahlyaytahss sahlahdhahss |
| cream | nata | nahtah |
| crisps | patatas fritas | pahtahtahss freetahss |
| cucumber | un pepino | oon paypeenoa |
| eggs | huevos | waybhoass |
| flour | harina | ahreenah |
| ham | jamón | khahmon |
| hamburgers | hamburguesas | ahmboorgayssahss |
| ice-cream | helado | aylahdhoa |
| lemons | unos limones | oonoass leemoanayss |
| lettuce | una lechuga | oonah lehchoogah |
| liver sausage | embutido de hígado | aymbooteedhoa day eegahdhoa |
| milk | leche | laychay |
| mustard | mostaza | moastahthah |
| oranges | naranjas | nahrahnkhahss |
| pâté | paté | pahtay |
| pepper | pimienta | peemyayntah |
| pickles | unos pepinillos | oonoass paypeeneelyoass |
| potato chips | patatas fritas | pahtahtahss freetahss |
| potatoes | unas patatas | oonahss pahtahtahss |
| rolls | unos panecillos | oonoass pahnaytheelyoass |
| salad | una ensalada | oonah aynsahlahdhah |
| salami | salchichón | sahlcheechon |

| salt | **sal** | sahl |
| sandwiches | **unos bocadillos** | oonoass boakahdheelyoass |
| sausages | **unas salchichas** | oonahss sahlcheechahss |
| spaghetti | **espaguetis** | ayspahgayteess |
| sugar | **azúcar** | ahthookahr |
| sweets | **unos caramelos** | oonoass kahrahmayloass |
| tea | **té** | tay |
| tomatoes | **unos tomates** | oonoass toamahtayss |

## And don't forget...

| a bottle opener | **un abridor de botellas** | oon ahbreedhor day boataylyahss |
| a corkscrew | **un sacacorchos** | oon sahkahkoarchoass |
| matches | **cerillas** | thayreelyahss |
| (paper) napkins | **servilletas (de papel)** | sehrbeelyaytahss (day pahpehl) |
| a tin (can) opener | **un abrelatas** | oon ahbraylahtahss |

### Weights and measures

1 kilogram or kilo (kg) = 1000 grams (g)

| 100 g = 3.5 oz. | ½ kg = 1.1 lb. |
| 200 g = 7.0 oz. | 1 kg = 2.2 lb. |

1 oz. = 28.35 g
1 lb. = 453.60 g

1 litre (l) = 0.88 imp. quarts = 1.06 U.S. quarts

| 1 imp. quart = 1.14 l | 1 U.S. quart = 0.95 l |
| 1 imp. gallon = 4.55 l | 1 U.S. gallon = 3.8 l |

| barrel | **el barril** | ayl bahrreel |
| box | **la caja** | lah kahkhah |
| can | **la lata** | lah lahtah |
| carton | **el cartón** | ayl kahrton |
| crate | **el cajón** | ayl kahkhon |
| jar | **el tarro** | ayl tahrroa |
| packet | **el paquete** | ayl pahkaytay |
| tin | **la lata** | lah lahtah |
| tube | **el tubo** | ayl toobhoa |

## Souvenirs

There's still a lot of local handicraft in Spain, and it may be worth your while to go and have a look at the products offered for sale in antique shops and on flea markets.

In some larger towns, there are shops called *Artesanía*. This is where the products of local craftsmen are sold. Ask for addresses at the tourist information office. Hand-made shawls, embroidered linen, lace-work, painted fans, hand-woven shopping baskets and many other items made of wickerwork and wood are produced for local consumption as well as the tourist trade.

Here are some more suggestions for articles which you may like to bring back as a souvenir or a gift:

| | | |
|---|---|---|
| bullfighter's cap | la montera | lah moantayrah |
| bullfight poster | el cartel de toros | ayl kahrtayl day toaroass |
| castanets | las castañuelas | lahss kahstahñwaylahss |
| cigarette box | la caja para cigarrillos | lah kahkhah pahrah theegahrreelynass |
| copperwork | los cobres | loss koabrayss |
| doll | la muñeca | lah moonaykah |
| earrings | los pendientes | loss payndyayntayss |
| earthenware | la loza de barro | lah loathah day bahrroa |
| embossed leather | el cuero repujado | ayl kwayroa raypookhah-dhoa |
| embroidery (hand-made) | el bordado (de artesanía) | ayl boardahdhoa (day ahrtayssahneeah) |
| fan | el abanico | ayl ahbhahneekoa |
| guitar | la guitarra | lah geetahrrah |
| jewelry | las joyas | lahss khoyahss |
| lace | los encajes | loss aynkahkhayss |
| mantilla | la mantilla | lah mahnteelyah |
| marzipan | el mazapán | ayl mahthahpahn |
| pitcher | el botijo | ayl boateekhoa |
| poncho | el poncho | ayl ponchoa |
| rosary | el rosario | ayl rossahryoa |
| shoes | los zapatos | loss thahpahtoass |
| suit | el traje | ayl trahkhay |
| suitcase | la maleta | lah mahlaytah |
| tambourine | la pandereta | lah pahndayraytah |
| wineskin | la bota | lah boatah |
| woodcarving | la carpintería | lah kahrpeentayreeah |

## Tobacconist's

Most Spanish cigarettes are made of strong, black tobacco.
They cost less than cigarettes in most other countries. Nearly
all major foreign brands are available in Spain at two to three
times the price of local cigarettes. The government tobacco
monopoly, Tabacalera S.A., operates shops and news-stands
in the country.

| | | |
|---|---|---|
| Give me a / an / some…, please. | Déme…, por favor. | daymay…por fahbhor |
| box of… | una caja de… | oonah kahkhah day |
| chewing tobacco | tabaco de mascar | tahbhahkoa day mahskahr |
| cigar | un puro | oon pooroa |
| cigars | unos puros | oonoass pooroass |
| cigarette case | una pitillera | oonah peeteelyayrah |
| cigarette holder | una boquilla | oonah boakeelyah |
| cigarette lighter | un encendedor | oon aynthayndaydhor |
| flints | unas piedras de mechero | oonahss pyaydrahss day maychayroa |
| lighter | un encendedor | oon aynthayndaydhor |
| lighter fluid | gasolina de encendedor | gahssoaleenah day aynthayndaydhor |
| lighter gas | gas para encendedor | gahss pahrah aynthayndaydhor |
| refill for a lighter | un repuesto para encendedor | oon rehpwaystoa pahrah aynthayndaydhor |
| matches | cerillas | thehreelyahss |
| packet of cigarettes | un paquete de cigarrillos | oon pahkaytay day theegahrreelyoass |
| packet of… | un paquete de… | oon pahkaytay day |
| pipe | una pipa | oonah peepah |
| pipe cleaners | unas escobillas | oonahss ayskoabheelyahss |
| pipe rack | un portapipas | oon portahpeepahss |
| pipe tobacco | tabaco de pipa | tahbhahkoa day peepah |
| pipe tool | utensillos auxiliares para pipa | ootaynseelyoass owkseelyahrayss pahrah peepah |
| snuff | rapé | rahpay |
| tobacco pouch | una tabaquera | oonah tahbhahkehrah |
| wick | una mecha | oonah maychah |

| | | |
|---|---|---|
| filter tipped | con filtro | kon feeltroa |
| without filter | sin filtro | seen feeltroa |
| king-size | extra largos | aystrah lahrgoass |

| Do you have any... cigarettes? | ¿Tiene usted cigarrillos...? | tyaynay oostaydh theegahrreelyoass |
|---|---|---|
| American | americanos | ahmayreekahnoass |
| English | ingleses | eenglayssayss |
| Spanish | españoles | ayspahñolayss |
| menthol | de mentol | day mayntol |
| I'll take two packets. | Me llevaré dos paquetes. | may lyaybhahray doss pahkaytayss |
| I'd like a carton. | Me llevaré un cartón. | may lyaybhahray oon kahrton |

While we're on the subject of cigarettes, suppose you want to offer somebody one?

| Would you like a cigarette? | ¿Quiero usted un cigarrillo? | kyayray oostaydh oon theegahrreelyna |
|---|---|---|
| Have one of mine. | Tome uno mío. | tomay oonon meena |
| Try one of these. | Pruebe uno de estos. | prwaybhay oonoa day aystoass |
| They're very mild. | Son muy suaves. | son mwee swahbhayss |
| They're a bit strong. | Son un poco fuertes. | son oon poakoa fwehr-tayss |

And if somebody offers you one?

| Thank you. | Gracias. | grahthyahss |
|---|---|---|
| No, thanks. | No, gracias. | noa grahthyahss |
| I don't smoke. | No fumo. | noa foomoa |
| I've given it up. | He dejado de fumar. | ay daykhahdhoa day foomahr |

# Your money: banks—currency

The normal banking hours in Spain are from 9 a.m. to 2 p.m. In banks in the larger towns there's sure to be someone who speaks English. In most tourist centres you'll find currency exchange offices *(cambio)*, especially during the summer season. The rates don't vary very much between them. They're often open outside regular banking hours and sometimes even on Sundays and holidays.

If stuck for a place to change money, check the railway station or try at your hotel. Remember to take your passport with you, since you may need it.

## Monetary unit

The basic unit of currency is the *peseta* (pay**ssay**tah), abbreviated *pta.* There are coins of 1, 5, 25 and 50 pesetas and banknotes of 100, 500, 1,000 and 5,000 pesetas.

## Before going

| | | |
|---|---|---|
| Where's the nearest bank? | ¿Dónde está el banco más cercano? | doanday aystah ayl bahnkoa mahss thehrkahnoa |
| Where's the nearest currency exchange? | ¿Dónde está la oficina de cambio más cercana? | doanday aystah lah oafeetheenah day kahmbyoa mahss thehrkahnah |
| What time does the bank open/close? | ¿A qué hora abren/cierran el banco? | ah kay oarah ahbrayn/thyehrrahn ayl bahnkoa |
| Where can I cash a traveller's cheque (check)? | ¿Dónde puedo cobrar un cheque de viajero? | doanday pwaydhoa koabrahr oon chehkay day byahkhayroa |
| Where's the Banco de Bilbao? | ¿Dónde está el Banco de Bilbao? | doanday aystah ayl bahnkoa day beelbahoa |

BANK

## Inside

| | | |
|---|---|---|
| I want to change some dollars / pounds. | Quiero cambiar unos dólares / unas libras esterlinas. | kyayroa kahmbyahr oonoass doalahrayss / oonahss leebrahss aystayrloenahss |
| Here's my passport. | Aquí está mi pasaporte. | ahkee aystah mee passahportay |
| What's the exchange rate? | ¿A cómo está el cambio? | ah koamoa aystah ayl kahmbyoa |
| What rate of commission do you charge? | ¿Qué comisión cargan? | kay koameessyon kahrgahn |
| Can you cash a personal choque? | ¿Puede hacer efectivo un cheque personal? | pwaydhay ahthehr ayfaykteebhoa oon chaykay pehrsoanahl |
| How long will it take to clear? | ¿Cuánto tardará en tramitarlo? | kwahntoa tahrdahrah ayn trahmeetahrloa |
| Can you wire my bank in London? | ¿Puede mandar un telegrama a mi banco en Londres? | pwaydhay mahndahr oon taylaygrahmah ah mee bahnkoa ayn londrayss |
| I have... | Tengo... | tayngoa |
| a letter of credit | una garantía bancaria | oonah gahrahnteeah bahnkohryah |
| an introduction from... | un formulario de presentación de... | oon formoolahryoa day prayssayntahthyon day... |
| a credit card | una tarjeta de crédito | oonah tahrkhaytah day kraydeetoa |
| I'm expecting some money from London. Has it arrived yet? | Espero una transferencia de Londres. ¿Ha llegado ya? | ayspayroa oonah trahnsfayraynthyah day londrayss. ah lyaygahdhoa yah |
| Please give me... notes (bills) and some small change. | Por favor, déme... billetes y algo en pequeño. | por fahbhor daymay... beelyaytayss ee ahlgoa ayn paykayñoa |
| Give me...large notes and the rest in small notes. | Déme... en los billetes de más valor que tenga y el resto en billetes de menor valor. | daymay...ayn loss beelyaytayss day mahss bahlor kay tayngah ee ayl raystoa ayn beelyaytayss day maynor bahlor |
| Could you please check that again? | ¿Podría comprobar de nuevo, por favor? | poadreeah koamproabhahr day nwaybhoa por fahbhor |

### Depositing

| | | |
|---|---|---|
| I want to credit this to my account. | **Quiero acreditar esto a mi cuenta.** | kyayroa ahkraydheetahr aystoa ah mee kwayntah |
| I want to credit this to Mr...'s account. | **Quiero acreditar esto a la cuenta del Señor...** | kyayroa ahkraydheetahr aystoa ah lah kwayntah dayl sayñor |
| Where should I sign? | **¿Dónde debo firmar?** | doanday daybhoa feermahr |

### Currency converter

In a world of fluctuating currencies, we can offer no more than this do-it-yourself chart. You can get a card showing current exchange rates from banks, travel agents and tourist offices. Why not fill in this chart, too, for handy reference?

| Spain | £ | $ |
|---|---|---|
| 1 peseta | | |
| 5 pesetas | | |
| 25 pesetas | | |
| 50 pesetas | | |
| 100 pesetas | | |
| 500 pesetas | | |
| 1,000 pesetas | | |

**BANK**

FOR NUMBERS, see page 175

# At the post-office

In Spain, post-offices are indicated by the words *Correos y Telégrafos*. The normal hours are from 9 a.m. to 2 p.m., Monday to Saturday. Some post-offices in the main towns are also open after hours.

If it's stamps you're after, you can also go to a tobacco shop. To post overseas mail, look for a box labelled *extranjero*.

| | | |
|---|---|---|
| Where's the nearest post-office? | ¿Dónde está la oficina de correos más cercana? | doanday aystah lah oafee-theenah day korrehoass mahss thehrkahnah |
| What time does the post-office open/close? | ¿A qué hora abren/cierran correos? | ah kay oarah ahbrayn/thyehrrahn korrehoass |
| What window do I go to for stamps? | ¿A qué ventanilla debo ir para comprar sellos? | ah kay bayntahneelyah daybhoa eer pahrah koamprahr saylyoass |
| At which counter can I cash an international money order? | ¿En qué mostrador puedo hacer efectivo un giro postal internacional? | ayn kay moastrahdhor pwaydhoa ahthehr ayfaykteebhoa oon kheeroa postahl oentehrnahthyonahl |
| I want some stamps, please. | Quiero unos sellos, por favor. | kyayroa oonoass saylyoass por fahbhor |
| I want...5-peseta stamps and...10-peseta stamps. | Quiero...sellos de 5 pesetas y...de 10 pesetas. | kyayroa...saylyoass day 5 payssaytahss ee...day 10 payssaytahss |
| What's the postage for a letter to London? | ¿Cuál es el franqueo para una carta para Londres? | kwahl ayss ayl frahnkehoa pahrah oonah kahrtah pahrah londrayss |
| What's the postage for a postcard to Los Angeles? | ¿Cuál es el franqueo para una tarjeta postal para Los Angeles? | kwahl ayss ayl frahnkehoa pahrah oonah tahrkhehtah postahl pahrah loss ahnkhaylayss |
| Do all letters go airmail? | ¿Van todas las cartas por vía aérea? | bahn toadhahss lahss kahrtahss por beeah ahayrehah |
| I want to send this parcel. | Quiero mandar este paquete. | kyayroa mahndahr aystay pahkaytay |

| Do I need to fill in a customs declaration ? | ¿Es necesario que cumplimente una declaración para la aduana ? | ayss naythayssahryoa kay koompleemayntay oonah dayklahrahthyon pahrah lah ahdwahnah |
| Where's the mailbox ? | ¿Dónde está el buzón ? | doanday aystah ayl boothon |
| I want to send this by... | Quiero mandar esto por... | kyayroa mahndahr aystoa por |
| airmail | correo aéreo | korrehoa ahayrehoa |
| express (special delivery) | urgente | oorkhayntay |
| registered mail | correo certificado | korrehoa thehrteefeekahdhoa |
| Where's the poste restante (general delivery) ? | ¿Dónde está la Lista de Correos ? | doanday aystah lah leestah day korrehoass |
| Is there any mail for me ? My name is... | ¿Hay correo para mí ? Me llamo... | igh korrehoa pahrah mee ? may lyahmoa |

| SELLOS | STAMPS |
| PAQUETES | PARCELS |
| GIROS POSTALES | MONEY ORDERS |

## Telegrams

In Spain, you'll have to go to the post-office to send a telegram. Some telegraph offices are open 24 hours a day.

| I want to send a telegram. May I please have a form ? | Quiero mandar un telegrama. ¿Me da un impreso, por favor ? | kyayroa mahndahr oon taylaygrahmah. may dah oon eemprehssoa por fahbhor |
| How much is it per word ? | ¿Cuánto cuesta por palabra ? | kwahntoa kwaystah por pahlahbrah |
| How long will a cable to Boston take ? | ¿Cuánto tardará un telegrama a Boston ? | kwahntoa tahrdahrah oon taylaygrahmah ah boston |
| I'd like to reverse the charges. | Quisiera que fuera con cobro revertido. | keessyayrah kay fwayrah kon koabroa raybhayrteedhoa |

## Telephoning

In all main towns, long-distance calls can be placed from telephone offices (usually distinct from post offices). Most hotels allow you to use their telephones for long-distance and international calls even if you aren't staying there. A small service charge is added to the charge ticket in such cases. The inland telephone network is partly automatic, and direct dialling is available to many countries.

### General

| | | |
|---|---|---|
| Where's the telephone? | ¿Dónde está el teléfono? | doanday aystah ayl taylayfoanoa |
| Where's the nearest telephone booth? | ¿Dónde está la cabina de teléfonos más cercana? | doanday aystah lah kahbheenah day taylayfoanoass mahss thehrkahnah |
| May I use your phone? | ¿Puedo usar su teléfono? | pwaydhoa oossahr soo taylayfoanoa |
| Do you have a telephone directory for Valladolid? | ¿Tiene usted una guía de teléfonos de Valladolid? | tyaynay oostaydh oonah geeah day taylayfoanoass day bahlyahdhoaleedh |
| Can you help me get this number? | ¿Me puede usted obtener este número? | may pwaydhay oostaydh obtehnayr aystay noomayroa |

### Operator

| | | |
|---|---|---|
| Do you speak English? | ¿Habla usted inglés? | ahblah oostaydh eenglayss |
| Good morning, I want Madrid 12 34 56. | Buenos días, quiero hablar con Madrid, número 12 34 56. | bwaynoass deeahss kyayroa ahblahr kon mahdreedh noomayroa 12 34 56 |

*Note:* Telephone numbers are given in pairs.

| | | |
|---|---|---|
| Can I dial direct? | ¿Puedo marcar directamente? | pwaydhoa mahrkahr deerayktahmayntay |
| I want to place a personal (person-to-person) call. | Quiero una llamada personal. | kyayroa oonah lyahmahdhah pehrsoanahl |

FOR NUMBERS, see page 175

TELEPHONE

| I want to reverse the charges. | Quiero que sea con cobro revertido. | kyayroa kay sehah kon koabroa raybhayrteedhoa |
| Will you tell me the cost of the call afterwards? | ¿Puede decirme el coste de la llamáda después? | pwaydhay daytheermay ayl koastay day lah lyah-mahdhah dayspwayss |

## Telephone alphabet

| | | | | | |
|---|---|---|---|---|---|
| A | **Antonio** | antoanyɵa | N | **Navarra** | nahbhahrrah |
| B | **Barcelona** | bahrthehloanah | Ñ | **Ñoño** | ñoañoa |
| C | **Carmen** | kahrmayn | O | **Oviedo** | oabhyaydhoa |
| CH | **Chocolate** | choakoalahtay | P | **París** | pahreess |
| D | **Dolores** | doaloarayss | Q | **Querido** | kayreedhoa |
| E | **Enrique** | aynreekay | R | **Ramón** | rahmon |
| F | **Francia** | frahnthyah | S | **Sábado** | sahbhahdhoa |
| G | **Gerona** | khehroanah | T | **Tarragona** | tahrrahgoanah |
| H | **Historia** | eestoaryah | U | **Ulises** | ooleessayss |
| I | **Inès** | eenayss | V | **Valencia** | bahlaynthyah |
| J | **José** | khoassay | W | **Washington** | wahzheenton |
| K | **Kilo** | keeloa | X | **Xiquena** | kseekaynah |
| L | **Lorenzo** | loaraynthoa | Y | **Yegua** | yehgwah |
| LL | **Llobregat** | lyoabraygaht | Z | **Zaragoza** | thahrahgothah |
| M | **Madrid** | mahdreedh | | | |

## Speaking

| Hello. This is... speaking. | Oíga. Aquí habla con... | oygah. ahkee ahblah kon |
| I want to speak to... | Quiero hablar con... | kyayroa ahblahr kon |
| Would you put me through to...? | ¿Querría comuni-carme con...? | kehrreeah koamoonee-kahrmay kon |
| I want extension... | Quisiera la exten-sión... | keessyayrah lah aykstayn-ssyon |
| Is this...? | ¿Es...? | ayss |

## Bad luck

| Would you please try again later? | ¿Querría intentarlo de nuevo más tarde? | kehrreeah eentayntahrloa day nwaybhoa mahss tahrday |

| Operator, you gave me the wrong number. | **Señorita, me ha dado el número equivocado.** | sayñoareetah may ah dahdhoa ayl noomayroa aykeebhoakahdhoa |
| Operator, we were cut off. | **Señorita, se nos ha cortado la línea.** | sayñoareetah say noas ah koartahdhoa lah leenayah |

## Not there

| When will he be back? | **¿Cuándo estará de vuelta?** | kwahndoa aystahrah day bwayltah |
| Will you tell him I called? My name's... | **Dígale que he llamado. Mi nombre es...** | deegahlay kay ay lyahmahdhoa. mee noambray ayss |
| Would you ask him to call me? | **¿Querría pedirle qué me llame?** | kehrreeah pehdheerlay kay may lyahmay |
| Would you please take a message? | **¿Por favor, quiere tomar un recado?** | por fahbhor kyayray toamahr oon raykahdhoa |

## Charges

| What was the cost of that call? | **¿Cuál ha sido el coste de esa llamada?** | kwahl ah soedhoa ayl koastay day ayssah lyahmahdhah |
| I want to pay for the call. | **Quiero pagar por la llamada.** | kyayroa pahgahr por lah lyahmahdhah |

---

| Hay una llamada para usted. | There's a telephone call for you. |
| ¿A qué número llama? | What number are you calling? |
| Comunica. | The line's engaged. |
| No contestan. | There's no answer. |
| Tiene el número equivocado. | You've got the wrong number. |
| El teléfono está estropeado. | The phone is out of order. |
| Ella no está ahora. | She's out at the moment. |

# The car

### Filling station

We'll start this section by considering your possible needs at a filling station. Most of them don't handle major repairs; but apart from providing you with fuel, they may be helpful in solving all kinds of minor problems.

| | | |
|---|---|---|
| Where's the nearest filling station? | ¿Dónde está la estación de servicio más cercana? | doanday aystah lah aystahthyon day sehrbee-thyoa mahss thehrkahnah |
| I want 20 litres of petrol (gas), please. | Quiero 20 litros de gasolina, por favor. | kyayroa 20 leetroass day gahssoaleenah por fahbhor |
| I want 30 litres of standard / premium. | Quiero 30 litros de la normal / de la super. | kyayroa 30 leetroass day lah normahl / day lah soopayr |
| Give me ... pesetas worth of petrol (gas). | Déme ... pesetas de gasolina. | daymay ... payssaytahss day gahssoaleenah |
| Full tank, please. | Llénelo, por favor. | lyaynayloa por fahbhor |
| Please check the oil and water. | Por favor, compruebe el aceite y el agua. | por fahbhor komprway-bhay ayl ahthaytay ee ayl ahgwah |
| Give me 2 litres of oil. | Déme 2 litros de aceite. | daymay 2 leetroass day ahthaytay |
| Fill up the battery with distilled water. | Llene la batería con agua destilada. | lyaynay lah bahtayreeah kon ahgwah daysteelah-dhah |
| Check the brake fluid. | Compruebe el líquido de frenos. | koamprwaybhay ayl leekeedhoa day fraynoass |

| Fluid measures | | | | | |
|---|---|---|---|---|---|
| litres | imp. gal. | U.S. gal. | litres | imp. gal. | U.S. gal. |
| 5 | 1.1 | 1.3 | 30 | 6.6 | 7.8 |
| 10 | 2.2 | 2.6 | 35 | 7.7 | 9.1 |
| 15 | 3.3 | 3.9 | 40 | 8.8 | 10.4 |
| 20 | 4.4 | 5.2 | 45 | 9.9 | 11.7 |
| 25 | 5.5 | 6.5 | 50 | 11.0 | 13.0 |

Tire pressure is measured in Spain in kilograms per square centimetre. The following conversion chart will make sure your tires get the treatment they deserve. Just point to the pressures required.

| Tire pressure | | | |
|---|---|---|---|
| lb./sq. in. | kg./cm² | lb./sq. in. | kg./cm² |
| 10 | 0.7 | 26 | 1.8 |
| 12 | 0.8 | 27 | 1.9 |
| 15 | 1.1 | 28 | 2.0 |
| 18 | 1.3 | 30 | 2.1 |
| 20 | 1.4 | 33 | 2.3 |
| 21 | 1.5 | 36 | 2.5 |
| 23 | 1.6 | 38 | 2.7 |
| 24 | 1.7 | 40 | 2.8 |

| | | |
|---|---|---|
| Would you check the tires? | ¿Quiere mirar los neumáticos? | kyayray moorahr loss nayoomahteekoass |
| 1.6 front, 1.8 rear. | 1,6 delanteras, 1,8 traseras. | 1 koamah 6 daylahntay-rahss 1 koamah 8 trahssayrahss |
| Please check the spare tire, too. | Mire la rueda de repuesto también, por favor. | meeray lah rwaydhah day raypwaystoa tahmbyayn por fahbhor |
| Can you mend this puncture (fix this flat)? | ¿Puede arreglar este pinchazo? | pwaydhay ahrrehglahr aystay peenchahthoa |
| Would you please change this tire? | ¿Puede cambiar esta rueda, por favor? | pwaydhay kahmbyahr aystah rwaydhah por fahbhor |
| Would you clean the windscreen (wind-shield)? | ¿Quiere limpiar el parabrisas? | kyayray leempyahr ayl pahrahbreessahss |
| Do you have a road map of this district? | ¿Tiene un mapa de carreteras de esta comarca? | tyaynay oon mahpah day kahrraytayrahss day aystah koamahrkah |
| Where are the toilets? | ¿Dónde están los lavabos? | doanday aystahn loss lahbhahbhoass |

## Asking the way—Street directions

| | | |
|---|---|---|
| Excuse me. | **Perdóneme.** | pehrdoanaymay |
| Can you tell me the way to...? | **¿Me puede decir cómo se va a...?** | may pwaydhay daytheer koamoa say bah ah |
| How do I get to...? | **¿Cómo se va a...?** | koamoa say bah ah |
| Where does this road lead to? | **¿Adónde lleva esta calle?** | ahdhoanday lyaybhah aystah kahlyay |
| Are we on the right road for...? | **¿Es ésta la carretera hacia...?** | ayss aystah lah kahrraytayrah ahthyah |
| How far is the next village? | **¿Qué distancia hay hasta el próximo pueblo?** | kay deestahnthyah igh ahstah ayl proakseemoa pwaybloa |
| How far is it to... from here? | **¿Qué distancia hay desde aquí hasta...?** | kay deestahnthyah igh daysday ahkee ahstah |
| Can you tell me where... is? | **¿Puede decirme dónde está...?** | pwaydhay daytheermay doanday aystah |
| Where can I find this address? | **¿Dónde queda esta dirección?** | doanday kaydhah aystah deerehkthyon |
| Where is this? | **¿Dónde está esto?** | doanday aystah aystoa |

### Miles into kilometres

1 mile = 1.609 kilometres (km.)

| miles | 10 | 20 | 30 | 40 | 50 | 60 | 70 | 80 | 90 | 100 |
|---|---|---|---|---|---|---|---|---|---|---|
| km. | 16 | 32 | 48 | 64 | 80 | 97 | 113 | 129 | 145 | 161 |

### Kilometres into miles

1 kilometre (km.) = 0.62 miles

| km. | 10 | 20 | 30 | 40 | 50 | 60 | 70 | 80 | 90 | 100 | 110 | 120 | 130 |
|---|---|---|---|---|---|---|---|---|---|---|---|---|---|
| miles | 6 | 12 | 19 | 25 | 31 | 37 | 44 | 50 | 56 | 62 | 68 | 75 | 81 |

| Can you show me on the map where I am? | ¿Puede enseñarme dónde estoy en el mapa? | pwaydhay aynsayñahrmay doanday aystoy ayn ayl mahpah |
| Can you show me on the map where the university is? | ¿Puede enseñarme dónde está la Universidad en el mapa? | pwaydhay aynsayñahrmay doanday aystah lah ooneebhehrseedhahdh ayn ayl mahpah |
| Can I park there? | ¿Se puede aparcar allí? | say pwaydhay ahpahrkahr ahlyee |
| Is that a one-way street? | ¿Es ésa una calle con sentido único? | ayss ayssah oonah kahlyay kon saynteedhoa ooneekoa |
| Does the traffic go this way? | ¿Circula el tráfico en este sentido? | theerkoolah ayl trahfeekoa ayn aystay saynteedhoa |

| | |
|---|---|
| Se ha equivocado usted de calle. | You're on the wrong road. |
| Siga todo derecho. | Go straight ahead. |
| Es hacia allí a... | It's down there on the... |
| la izquierda/la derecha | left/right |
| Vaya al primer/segundo cruce. | Go to the first/second crossroads. |
| Doble a la izquierda en el semáforo. | Turn left at the traffic lights. |
| Doble a la derecha en la próxima esquina. | Turn right at the next corner. |

CAR—INFORMATION

In the rest of this section, we'll be more closely concerned with the car itself. We've divided it into two parts:

*Part A* contains general advice on motoring in Spain. It's essentially for reference and is therefore to be browsed over, preferably in advance.

*Part B* is concerned with the practical details of accidents and breakdown. It includes a list of car parts and a list of things that may go wrong with them. All you have to do is to show it to the garage mechanic and get him to point to the items required.

## Part A

### Customs—Documentation

You'll need the following documents when driving in Spain:

passport
international insurance certificate (green card)
registration (log) book
valid driving licence

The nationality plate or sticker must be on the car. Since some countries require a translation of your home driving licence, an international driving permit may save you trouble; but in Spain you can drive with a British or American driving licence.

A red warning triangle—for display on the road in case of accident—is compulsory; so is the use of seat belts outside city limits. Crash helmets must be worn by both riders and passengers on motorcycles and scooters.

| Here's my... | Aquí está mi... | ahkee aystah mee |
|---|---|---|
| driving licence | **carnet de conducir** | kahrnay day kondootheer |
| green card | **carta verde** | kahrtah behrday |
| passport | **pasaporte** | pahssahportay |
| registration book | **certificado de matrícula** | thehrteefeekahdhoa day mahtreekoolah |

CAR—INFORMATION

| I haven't anything to declare. | **No tengo nada que declarar.** | noa **tayngoa nahdhah** kay dayklah**rahr** |
| I've... | **Tengo...** | **tayngoa** |
| a carton of cigarettes | **un cartón de cigarrillos** | oon kahr**ton** day theegahr**reelyoass** |
| a bottle of whisky | **una botella de whisky** | oonah boa**taylyah** day **weeskee** |
| a bottle of wine | **una botella de vino** | oonah boa**taylyah** day **beenoa** |
| We're staying for... | **Nos quedaremos..** | noss kayd**hahraymoass** |
| three days | **tres días** | trayss **deeahss** |
| a week | **una semana** | oonah say**mahnah** |
| two weeks | **dos semanas** | doss say**mahnahss** |
| a month | **un mes** | oon **mayss** |

## Driving

The classification of roads in Spain is as follows:

| N. IV | Main through road, starting from Madrid (national road) |
| N. 4 | All other main roads |
| C. 2 | Second-class country roads |

Arterial roads are generally very good, with long stretches in the open country virtually deserted. On certain routes, however, heavy commercial traffic often clogs inadequate two-lane highways. Spain's expanding motorway (expressway) network is excellently engineered, but rather expensive tolls are charged. Unclassified country roads can be in very poor driving condition.

If you're driving inland, you should remember that petrol (gas) stations are not so prevalent as on the coasts; it's a good thing to take a jerrycan of petrol with you. Take a bottle of distilled water for the battery as well, if you're driving in summer. A set of spare parts obtainable from car dealers is also recommended.

You'll notice that the Spanish—who are good, though somewhat emotional, drivers—have a habit of honking much more than seems necessary. The country roads are often crowded with donkeys, cattle and farmer's carts, however, which may come into view only at the last moment—like after a curve or a hilltop. So drive carefully and don't hesitate to honk in situations where the visibility is obstructed.

The police are normally quite lenient with tourists, but don't push your luck too far. For small offences you can be fined on the spot. Here are some phrases which may come in handy in the case of confrontation with the *Guardia Civil*. If you're in serious trouble, insist on an interpreter.

| | | |
|---|---|---|
| I'm sorry, I didn't see the sign. | Lo siento, no he visto la indicación. | loa **syayn**toa noa ay **bees**toa lah eendeekah**thyon** |
| The light was green. | El semáforo estaba en verde. | ayl saymah**fo**roa aystah**bh**ah ayn **behr**day |
| I don't understand. | No entiendo. | noa ayn**tyayn**doa |
| How much is the fine? | ¿Cuánto es la multa? | **kwahn**toa ayss lah **mool**tah |

## Parking

Use your common sense when parking. Park your vehicle in the direction of moving traffic, not against it. Obey the parking regulations, which will be indicated by signs or by red and white lines painted on the edge of the pavement (sidewalk).

| | | |
|---|---|---|
| Excuse me. May I park here? | Perdone. ¿Puedo aparcar aquí? | pehr**doa**nay. **pway**dhoa ahpahr**kahr** ah**kee** |
| How long can I park here? | ¿Cuánto tiempo puedo aparcar aquí? | **kwahn**toa **tyaym**poa **pway**dhoa ahpahr**kahr** ah**kee** |
| What's the charge for parking here? | ¿Cuánto cuesta aparcar aquí? | **kwahn**toa **kways**tah ahpahr**kahr** ah**kee** |
| Do I have to leave my lights on? | ¿Tengo que dejar las luces encendidas? | **tayn**goa kay deh**khahr** lahss **loo**thayss aynthayn**deed**hahss |
| Excuse me. Do you have some change for the parking meter? | Perdone. ¿Tiene suelto para el parquímetro? | pehr**doa**nay. **tyay**nay **sway**ltoa pahrah ayl pahr**kee**mehtroa |

## Road signs

Road signs are practically standardized throughout Western Europe. You should learn to recognize them, particularly those shown on pages 160 and 161.

Listed below are the main written signs which you may encounter when driving through Spain.

| | |
|---|---|
| ADUANA | Customs |
| AL PASO | Drive slowly |
| ¡ALTO! | Stop |
| APARCAMIENTO | Parking lot |
| ATENCION | Caution |
| AUTOPISTA (DE PEAJE) | Motorway/Turnpike (with toll) |
| CALZADA DETERIORADA | Bad road surface |
| CAÑADA | Road narrows |
| CARRETERA CORTADA | No through road |
| CEDA EL PASO | Give way (yield) |
| CENTRO URBANO | City centre |
| CRUCE PELIGROSO | Dangerous crossroads |
| CUIDADO | Caution |
| CURVA PELIGROSA | Dangerous bend (curve) |
| DESPACIO | Slow |
| DESVIACION | Diversion (detour) |
| DIRECCION PROHIBIDA | No entry |
| DIRECCION UNICA | One-way street |
| ENCENDER LAS LUCES | Turn on headlights |
| ESCUELA | School |
| ESTACIONAMIENTO PROHIBIDO | No parking |
| ESTACIONAMIENTO REGLAMENTADO | Limited parking zone |
| FUERTE DECLIVE | Steep incline |
| OBRAS | Road works (men working) |
| PASO DE GANADO | Cattle crossing |
| PASO A NIVEL | Level (railroad) crossing |
| PASO PROHIBIDO | No entry |
| PEATONES | Pedestrians |
| PELIGRO | Danger |
| PROHIBIDO ADELANTAR | No overtaking (passing) |
| PROHIBIDO EL PASO | No entry |
| PUESTO DE SOCORRO | First-aid |
| SALIDA DE FABRICA | Factory exit |
| ZONA AZUL | Limited parking zone |

CAR—INFORMATION

## Part B

## Accidents

This section is confined to immediate aid. The legal problems of responsibility and settlement can be taken care of at a later stage. Your first concern will be for the injured.

| Is anyone hurt? | ¿Hay algún herido? | igh ahl**goon** ehreedhoa |
| Don't move. | No se mueva. | noa say **mway**bhah |
| It's all right. Don't worry. | Todo está bien. No se preocupe. | **toa**dhoa aystah byayn. noa say prehoako**opay** |
| Where's the nearest telephone? | ¿Dónde está el teléfono más cercano? | **doan**day aystah ayl taylayfoanoa mahss thehr-**kah**noa |
| Can I use your telephone? There's been an accident. | ¿Puedo usar su teléfono? Ha ha-bido un accidente. | **pway**dhoa oossahr soo taylayfoanoa? ah ah**bhee**-dhoa oon aktheedayntay |
| Call a doctor/an ambulance quickly. | Llamen a un doctor/una ambulancia. | **lyah**mayn ah oon doaktor/ oonah ahmboolahn**thyah** |
| There are people injured. | Hay gente herida. | igh **khayn**tay ehreedhah |
| Help me get them out of the car. | Ayúdeme a sacarlos del coche. | ah**yoo**dhaymay ah sah**kahr**-loass dayl **koa**chay |

## Police—Exchange of information

| Please call the police. | Llamen a la policía, por favor. | **lyah**mayn ah lah poalee-**theeah** por fah**bhor** |
| There's been an accident. It's about 2 km. from... | Ha habido un accidente. Está a unos 2 kilómetros de... | ah ah**bhee**dhoa oon ahktheedhayntay. aystah ah oonoass 2 keeloamehtroass day |
| I'm on the Gerona–Barcelona road, 25 kilometres from Barcelona. | Estoy en la carre-tera de Gerona a Barcelona, a 25 kilómetros de Barcelona. | ay**stoy** ayn lah kahrray-tayrah day khay**roa**nah ah bahrthay**loa**nah ah 25 keeloamehtroass day bahrthay**loa**nah |
| Here's my name and address. | Estos son mi nombre y dirección. | **ays**toass son mee **noam**bray ee deerayk**thyon** |

| Would you mind acting as a witness? | ¿Quisiera usted servir de testigo? | keessyayrah oostaydh sehrbeer day taysteegoa |
| I'd like an interpreter. | Quisiera un intérprete. | keessyayrah oon eentehrpraytay |

Remember to put out a red warning triangle if the car is out of action or impeding traffic.

## Breakdown

...and that's what we'll do with this section: break it down into four phases.

1. *On the road*
   You ask where the nearest garage is.

2. *At the garage*
   You tell the mechanic what's wrong.

3. *Finding the trouble*
   He tells you what he thinks is wrong.

4. *Getting it repaired*
   You tell him to repair it and, once that's over, settle the account (or argue about it).

### Phase 1—On the road

| Where's the nearest garage? | ¿Dónde está el garage más cercano? | doanday aystah ayl gahrahkhay mahss thehrkahnoa |
| Excuse me. My car has broken down. May I use your phone? | Perdóneme. Mi coche se ha estropeado. ¿Puedo usar su teléfono? | pehrdoanaymay. mee koachay say ah aystroapehahdhoa. pwaydhoa oossahr soo taylayfoanoa |
| What's the telephone number of the nearest garage? | ¿Cuál es el número de teléfono del garage más cercano? | kwahl ayss ayl noomayroa day taylayfoanoa dayl gahrahkhay mahss thehrkahnoa |
| I've had a breakdown at... | Tengo un coche estropeado en... | tayngoa oon koachay aystroapehahdhoa ayn |
| Can you send a mechanic? | ¿Puede usted mandar un mecánico? | pwaydhay oostaydh mahndahr oon maykahneekoa |

| Can you send a truck to tow my car? | ¿Puede usted mandar una grúa para remolcar mi coche? | pwaydhay oostaydh mahndahr oonah grooah pahrah raymoalkahr mee koachay |
| How long will you be? | ¿Cuánto tardarán? | kwahntoa tahrdahrahn |

## Phase 2—At the garage

| Can you help me? | ¿Puede usted ayudarme? | pwaydhay oostaydh ahyoodhahrmay |
| I don't know what's wrong with it. | No sé lo que le pasa. | noa say loa kay lay pahssan |
| I think there's something wrong with the... | Creo que hay algo que no va bien en... | krehoa kay igh ahlgoa kay noa bah byayn ayn |
| automatic transmission | transmisión automática | trahnsmeethyon owtoamah-teekah |
| battery | batería | bahtayreeah |
| brakes | frenos | frehnoass |
| bulbs | bombillas | boambeelyahss |
| carburettor | carburador | kahrboorahdhor |
| clutch | embrague | aymbrahgay |
| contact | contacto | kontahktoa |
| cooling system | sistema de enfriamiento | seestaymah day aynfreeah-myayntoa |
| dipswitch (dimmers) | luces bajas | loothayss bahkhahss |
| dynamo | generador | khaynayrahdhor |
| electrical system | sistema eléctrico | seestaymah aylehktreekoa |
| engine | motor | moatoar |
| exhaust pipe | tubo de escape | toobhoa day ayskahpay |
| fan | ventilación | baynteelahthyon |
| filter | filtro | feeltroa |
| fuel pump | bomba de gasolina | boambah day gahssoaleenah |
| fuel tank | depósito | daypoasseetoa |
| gears | caja de cambios | kahkhah day kahmbyoass |
| generator | generador | khaynayrahdhor |
| headlights | luces de cruce | loothayss day kroothay |
| heating | calefacción | kahlayfahthyon |
| horn | klaxón | klahkson |
| ignition system | encendido | aynthayndeedhoa |
| lights | luces | loothayss |
| reversing (back-up) lights | luz de marcha atrás | looth day mahrchah ahtrahss |

| brake lights | **luz del freno** | looth dayl **frehnoa** |
| rear (tail) lights | **luces traseras** | **loothayss** trah**ssayrahss** |
| lines | **cables** | **kahblayss** |
| lining and covering | **tapizado** | tahpee**thahdhoa** |
| lubrication system | **sistema** | seestaymah day loobreefee- |
| | **de lubrificación** | **kathyon** |
| parking brake | **freno de estaciona-** | frehnoa day aystahthyonah- |
| | **miento** | **myayntoa** |
| radiator | **radiador** | rahdhyah**dhor** |
| reflectors | **reflectores** | rehflayk**toarayss** |
| seat | **asiento** | ah**ssyayntoa** |
| sliding roof | **techo deslizante** | taychoa daysleethahntay |
| sparking plugs | **bujías** | book**heeahss** |
| speedometer | **indicador de** | eendeekahdhor day behloa- |
| | **velocidad** | theedhahdh |
| starter | **motor de arranque** | moator day ahrrahnkay |
| (power) steering | **(servo-) dirección** | (sehrboa-) deeraykthyon |
| suspension | **suspensión** | soospaynsyon |
| turn signal | **indicador de direc-** | eendeekahdhor day |
| | **ción** | deeraykthyon |
| wheels | **ruedas** | **rwaydhahss** |
| wipers | **limpiaparabrisas** | leempyahpahrahbreessahss |

| RIGHT | LEFT | FRONT | BACK |
|---|---|---|---|
| **DERECHA** | **IZQUIERDA** | **DELANTE** | **DETRAS** |
| (dayraychah) | (eethkyayrdah) | (daylahntay) | (daytrahss) |

| It's... | **Está...** | aystah |
|---|---|---|
| bad | **mal** | mahl |
| blowing | **ventilando** | baynteelahndoa |
| blown | **pinchado** | peenchahdhoa |
| broken | **roto** | roatoa |
| burnt | **quemado** | kaymahdhoa |
| cracked | **resquebrajado** | rehskaybrahkhahdhoa |
| defective | **defectivo** | dayfehkteebhoa |
| disconnected | **desconectado** | deskoanayktahdhoa |
| dry | **seco** | sehkoa |
| frozen | **helado** | aylahdhoa |
| jammed | **atascado** | ahtahskahdhoa |
| knocking | **golpeando** | goalpehahndoa |
| leaking | **goteando** | goatehahndoa |
| loose | **suelto** | swayltoa |
| misfiring | **fallando** | fahlyahndoa |
| noisy | **ruidoso** | rweedhoassoa |

| | | |
|---|---|---|
| short-circuiting | **fundiendo** | foon**dyayn**doa |
| slack | **flojo** | **floa**khoa |
| slipping | **resbaladizo** | raysbahlah**dhee**thoa |
| stuck | **atascado** | ahtah**skahdh**oa |
| vibrating | **vibrando** | bee**brahn**doa |
| weak | **débil** | **dehb**heel |
| worn | **gastado** | gah**stahdh**oa |

| | | |
|---|---|---|
| It's overheating. | **Calienta demasiado.** | kah**lyayn**tha daymah**ssyahdh**oa |
| It's not working. | **No funciona.** | noa foonk**thyo**nah |
| The car won't start. | **El coche no arranca.** | ayl **koa**chay noa ah**rrahn**kah |
| It's locked and the keys are inside. | **Está cerrado con llave y las llaves han quedado dentro.** | ay**stah** ther**rahdh**oa kon **lyahb**hay ee lahss **lyahb**hayss ahn kay**dhahdh**oa **dayn**troa |
| The radiator is leaking. | **El radiador tiene un escape.** | ayl rahdh**yahdh**or **tyay**nay oon ay**skah**pay |
| I want maintenance and lubrication service. | **Quiero servicio de revisión y engrase.** | **kyay**roa sehr**bee**thyoa day raybhee**thyon** ee ayn**grahss**ay |
| The clutch engages too quickly. | **El embrague embraga demasiado rápido.** | ayl aym**brah**gay aym**brah**gah daymah**ssyahdh**oa **rah**peedhoa |
| The steering wheel is vibrating. | **El volante vibra.** | ayl boa**lahn**tay **bee**brah |
| The wipers are smearing. | **Los limpiaparabrisas están sucios.** | loss leempyahpahrahb**ree**ssahss ay**stahn soo**thyoass |
| The pneumatic suspension is weak. | **La suspensión neumática es débil.** | lah soospayn**syon** nayoo**mah**teekah ayss **dayb**heel |
| The...needs adjusting. | **... necesita ajuste.** | ...naythay**ssee**tah ah**khoo**stay |

Now that you've explained what's wrong, you'll want to know how long it will take to repair it and make your arrangements accordingly.

| | | |
|---|---|---|
| How long will it take to repair? | **¿Cuánto tiempo tardará en repararlo?** | **kwahn**toa **tyaym**poa tahr**dah**rah ayn raypah**rahr**loa? |

| How long will it take to find out what's wrong? | ¿Cuánto tardarán en encontrar la avería? | kwahntoa tahrdahrahn ayn aynkoantrahr lah ahbhayreeah |
| Suppose I come back in half an hour? | ¿Podré volver en media hora? | poadray boalbayr ayn mehdhyah oarah |
| Can you give me a lift into town? | ¿Puede usted llevarme hasta la ciudad? | pwaydhay oostaydh lyaybhahrmay ahstah lah thyoodhahdh |

## Phase 3—Finding the trouble

If you don't know what's wrong with the car, it's up to the mechanic to find the trouble. You can ask him what has to be repaired by handing him the book and pointing to the Spanish text below.

**Haga el favor de mirar la lista alfabética e indique el elemento defectivo. Si el cliente quiere saber cuál es la avería, escoja la palabra de la lista siguiente (roto, corto-circuitado, etc.).\***

| agua destilada | distilled water |
| amortiguador | shock absorber |
| árbol de levas | camshaft |
| armadura del motor de arranque | starter armature |
| batería | battery |
| bloque | block |
| bobina | ignition coil |
| bomba | pump |
| bomba de agua | water pump |
| bomba de gasolina | petrol (fuel) pump |
| bomba de inyección | injection pump |
| bujías | sparking plugs |
| cable | cable |
| cables de bujías | sparking-plug leads |
| cable del distribuidor | distributor lead |
| caja de cambios | gear box |
| caja de dirección | steering box |

\* Please look at the following alphabetical list and point to the defective item. If your customer wants to know what's wrong with it, pick the applicable term from the next list (broken, short-circuited, etc.).

CAR—REPAIRS

| | |
|---|---|
| carburador | carburettor |
| cárter | crankcase |
| células de la batería | battery cells |
| cigüeñal | crankshaft |
| cilindro | cylinder |
| cojinetes | main bearings |
| columna de dirección | steering column post |
| condensador | condensor |
| conexión | connection |
| contacto | contact |
| correa del ventilador | fan belt |
| culata | cylinder head |
| diafragma | diaphragm |
| dientes | teeth |
| dirección | steering |
| disco del embrague | clutch plate |
| distribuidor | distributor |
| eje | shaft |
| embrague | clutch |
| engranaje | gear |
| escobillas | brushes |
| estabilizador | stabilizer |
| filtro | filter |
| filtro de aire | air filter |
| filtro/bomba de aceite | oil filter/pump |
| filtro de gasolina | petrol filter |
| flotador | float |
| forro | lining |
| freno | break |
| generador | dynamo (generator) |
| grasa | grease |
| interruptor de luces | dipswitch (dimmer switch) |
| junta | joint |
| junta de la culata | cylinder head gasket |
| junta principal | universal joint |
| líquido de la batería | battery liquid |
| motor | engine |
| motor de arranque | starter motor |
| muelle de la válvula | valve spring |
| muelles | springs |
| muelles del embrague | pressure springs |
| pedal del embrague | clutch pedal |
| piñón de ataque | rack and pinion |
| pistón | piston |
| platinos | points |
| radiador | radiator |

| | |
|---|---|
| rótulas de la barra de acoplamiento | track-rod ends |
| ruedas | wheels |
| segmentos | rings |
| segmentos del pistón | piston rings |
| sistema de enfriamiento | cooling system |
| sistema eléctrico | electrical system |
| soporte | bearing |
| suspensión | suspension |
| suspensión hidroneumática | pneumatic suspension |
| tambor del freno | brake drum |
| termostato | thermostat |
| transmisión | transmission |
| transmisión automática | automatic transmission |
| tubos | stems |
| válvula | valve |
| varillas | tappets |
| ventilador | fan |
| zapata | shoes |

**La lista siguiente contiene palabras que describen lo que ocurre, así como la reparación que es necesario hacer.***

| | |
|---|---|
| aflojar | to loosen |
| ajustar | to adjust |
| alabeado | warped |
| alto | high |
| apretar | to tighten |
| atascado | stuck/jammed |
| bajo | low |
| calentando demasiado | overheating |
| cambiar | to change |
| cargar | to charge |
| corroído | corroded |
| defectivo | defective |
| desconectado | disconnected |
| desmontar | to strip down |
| engranar | to grind in |
| equilibrar | to balance |
| escapar | to bleed |
| fallando | misfiring |
| flojo | weak/slack |
| fundido | short-circuited |
| golpeando | knocking |

* The following list contains words which describe what's wrong as well as what may need to be done.

| | |
|---|---|
| goteando | leaking |
| hacer juego | play |
| helado | frozen |
| limpiar | to clean |
| pinchado | blown |
| pinchazo | puncture |
| quemado | burnt |
| rápido | quick |
| reajustar | to reline |
| reemplazar | to replace |
| resbaladizo | slipping |
| resquebrajado | cracked |
| roto | broken |
| seco | dry |
| sucio | dirty |
| suelto | loose |
| ventilando | blowing |
| vibrando | vibrating |

## Phase 4—Getting it repaired

| | | |
|---|---|---|
| Have you found the trouble? | ¿Ha encontrado usted la avería? | ah aynkoantrahdhoa oostaydh lah ahbhayreeah |

Now that you know what's wrong, or at least have some idea, you'll want to find out…

| | | |
|---|---|---|
| Is that serious? | ¿Es eso grave? | ayss ayssoa grahbhay |
| Can you repair it? | ¿Puede repararlo? | pwaydhay raypahrahrloa |
| What's it going to cost? | ¿Cuánto me va a costar? | kwahntoa may bah ah koastahr |
| Do you have the necessary spare parts? | ¿Tiene las piezas de recambio necesarias? | tyaynay lahss pyehthahss day rehkahmbyoa naythayssahryahss |

## What if he says "no"?

| | | |
|---|---|---|
| Why can't you do it? | ¿Por qué no puede hacerlo? | por kay noa pwaydhay ahthehrloa |
| Is it essential to have that part? | ¿Es imprescindible que tenga esa pieza? | ayss eempraystheendeeblay kay tayngah ayssah pyehtah |

| How long is it going to take to get the spare parts? | ¿Cuánto demorará en conseguir las piezas de recambio? | kwahntoa daymoarahrah ayn koansaygeer lahss pyehthahss day rehkahmbyoa |
| Where's the nearest garage that can repair it? | ¿Cuál es el garage más cercano que puede repararlo? | kwahl ayss ayl gahrahkhay mahss thehrkahnoa kay pwaydhay raypahrahrloa |
| Can you fix it so that I can get as far as...? | ¿Puede hacer una reparación provisional de modo que pueda llegar a...? | pwaydhay ahthehr oonah raypahrahthyon probhee-ssyonahl day moadhoa kay pwaydhah lyaygahr ah |

If you're really stuck, ask if you can leave the car at the garage. Contact an automobile association or hire another car.

### Settling the bill

| Is everything fixed? | ¿Ya está todo arreglado? | yah aystah toadhoa ahrrehglahdhoa |
| How much do I owe you? | ¿Cuánto le debo? | kwahntoa lay daybhoa |
| Will you take a traveller's cheque? | ¿Me acepta usted un cheque de viajero? | may ahthayptah oostaydh oon chaykay day byahkhehroa |
| Thanks very much for your help. | Muchas gracias por su ayuda. | moochahss grahthyahss por soo ahyoodhah |
| This is for you. | Esto es para usted. | aystoa ayss pahrah oostaydh |

But you may feel that the workmanship is sloppy or that you are paying for work not done. Get the bill itemized. If necessary, get it translated before you pay.

| I'd like to check the bill first. Will you itemize the work done? | Quisiera comprobar la factura primero. ¿Podría especificar el trabajo realizado? | keessyayrah komproabhar lah fahktoorah preemayroa. poadreeah ayspaytheefee-kahr ayl trahbahkhoa rehahleethahdhoa |

If the garage still won't back down and you're sure you're right, get the help of a third party.

# Some international road signs

No vehicles

No entry

No overtaking
(passing)

Oncoming traffic
has priority

Maximum
speed limit

No parking

Caution

Intersection

Dangerous bend
(curve)

Road narrows

Intersection
with secondary
road

Two-way traffic

Dangerous hill

Uneven road

Falling rocks

Give way (yield)

Main road, thoroughfare

End of restriction

One-way traffic

Traffic goes this way

Roundabout (rotary)

Bicycles only

Pedestrians only

Minimum speed limit

Keep right (left if symbol reversed)

Parking

Hospital

Motorway (expressway)

Motor vehicles only

Filling station

No through road

# Doctor

Frankly, how much use is a phrase book going to be to you in case of serious injury or illness? The only phrase you need in such an emergency is…

| | | |
|---|---|---|
| Get a doctor quickly! | ¡Traigan un médico rápidamente! | trighgahn oon mehdheekoa rahpeedhahmayntay |

But there are minor aches and pains, ailments and irritations that can upset the best-planned trip. Here we can help you and, perhaps, the doctor.

Some doctors will speak English well; others will know enough for your needs. But suppose there's something the doctor can't explain because of language difficulties? We've thought of that. As you'll see, this section has been arranged to enable you and the doctor to communicate. From pages 165 to 171, you find your part of the dialogue on the upper half of each page—the doctor's is on the lower half.

The whole section has been divided into three parts: illness, wounds, nervous tension. Page 171 is concerned with prescriptions and fees.

### General

| | | |
|---|---|---|
| I need a doctor—quickly. | Necesito un médico —rápidamente. | naythaysseetoa oon mehdheekoa rahpeedhahmayntay |
| Can you get me a doctor? | ¿Puede usted buscarme un médico? | pwaydhay oostaydh booskahrmay oon mehdheekoa |
| Is there a doctor here? | ¿Hay un médico aquí? | igh oon mehdheekoa ahkee |
| Please telephone for a doctor immediately. | Por favor, llame al médico inmediatamente. | por fahbhor lyahmay ahl mehdheekoa eenmaydhyahtahmayntay |
| Where's there a doctor who speaks English? | ¿Dónde hay un médico que hable inglés? | doanday igh oon mehdheekoa kay ahblay eenglayss |

| Is there an American hospital in town? | ¿Hay un hospital americano en la ciudad? | igh oon oaspeetahl ahmayreekahnoa ayn lah thyoodhahdh |
| Where's the surgery (doctor's office)? | ¿Dónde es la consulta? | doanday ayss lah koansooltah |
| What are the surgery (office) hours? | ¿Cuáles son las horas de consulta? | kwahlayss son lahss oarahss day koansooltah |
| Could the doctor come to see me here? | ¿Podría el médico venir a reconocerme aquí? | poadreeah ayl mehdheekoa behneer ah rehkoanoathehrmay ahkee |
| What time can the doctor come? | ¿A qué hora puede venir el médico? | ah kay oarah pwaydhay bayneer ayl mehdheekoa |

## Symptoms

Use this section to tell the doctor what's wrong. Basically, what he'll need to know is:

**What?** (ache, pain, bruise, etc.)
**Where?** (arm, stomach, etc.)
**How long?** (have you had the trouble)

Before you visit the doctor, find out the answers to these questions by glancing through the pages that follow. In this way, you'll save time.

## Parts of the body

| ankle | tobillo | toabeelyoa |
| appendix | apéndice | ahpayndeethay |
| arm | brazo | brahthoa |
| artery | arteria | ahrtayreeah |
| bladder | vesícula | baysseekoolah |
| blood | sangre | sahngray |
| bone | hueso | wayssoa |
| cheek | mejilla | maykheelyah |
| chest | pecho | pehchoa |
| chin | barbilla | bahrbeelyah |
| collar bone | clavícula | klahbheekoolah |
| ear | oreja | oarehkhah |
| elbow | codo | koadhoa |
| eye | ojo | oakhoa |

DOCTOR

| | | |
|---|---|---|
| face | **cara** | kahrah |
| finger | **dedo** | daydhoa |
| foot | **pie** | pyay |
| forehead | **frente** | frayntay |
| gland | **glándula** | glahndoolah |
| hair | **pelo** | payloa |
| hand | **mano** | mahnoa |
| head | **cabeza** | kahbhaythah |
| heart | **corazón** | koarahthon |
| heel | **talón** | tahlon |
| hip | **cadera** | kahdhehrah |
| intestines | **intestinos** | eentaysteenoass |
| jaw | **mandíbula** | mahndeebhoolah |
| joint | **articulación** | ahrteekoolahthyon |
| knee | **rodilla** | roadheelyah |
| knee cap | **rótula** | rotoolah |
| leg | **pierna** | pyehrnah |
| lip | **labio** | lahbhyoa |
| liver | **hígado** | eegahdhoa |
| lung | **pulmón** | poolmon |
| mouth | **boca** | boakah |
| muscle | **músculo** | mooskooloa |
| neck | **cuello** | kwaylyoa |
| nerve | **nervio** | nehrbyoa |
| nervous system | **sistema nervioso** | seestaymah nehrbyoassoa |
| nose | **nariz** | nahreeth |
| rib | **costilla** | koasteelyah |
| shoulder | **espalda** | ayspahldah |
| skin | **piel** | pyayl |
| spine | **columna** | koaloomnah |
| stomach | **estómago** | aystoamahgoa |
| tendon | **tendón** | tayndon |
| thigh | **muslo** | moosloa |
| throat | **garganta** | gahrgahntah |
| toe | **dedo del pie** | daydhoa dayl pyay |
| tongue | **lengua** | layngwah |
| tonsils | **amígdalas** | ahmeegdahlahss |
| urine | **orina** | oareenah |
| vein | **vena** | baynah |
| wrist | **muñeca** | mooñaykah |

| | |
|---|---|
| left/on the left side | right/on the right side |
| **izquierdo/ a izquierda** | **derecho/ a derecha** |
| (eethkyayrdoa/ah eethkyayrdah) | (dayraychoa/ah dayraychah) |

# PATIENT

## Part 1—Illness

| | | |
|---|---|---|
| I'm not feeling well. | **No me encuentro bien.** | noa may aynkwayntroa byayn |
| I'm ill. | **Estoy enfermo/ enferma.** | aystoy aynfehrmoa/ aynfehrmah |
| I've got a pain here. | **Tengo un dolor aquí.** | tayngoa oon doalor ahkee |
| His/Her...hurts. | **Su...le duele.** | soo...lay dwaylay |
| I've got (a)... | **Tengo...** | tayngoa |
| headache | **dolor de cabeza** | doalor day kahbhaythah |
| backache | **dolor de espalda** | doalor day ayspahldah |
| fever | **fiebre** | fyehbray |
| sore throat | **garganta irritada** | gahrgahntah eerreetahdhah |
| travel sickness | **el mareo** | ayl mahrehoa |
| I'm constipated. | **Estoy estreñido.** | aystoy aystrehñeedhoa |
| I've been vomiting. | **He tenido vómitos.** | ay tayneedhoa boameetoass |

DOCTOR

---

# DOCTOR

## Malestares y dolores

| | |
|---|---|
| ¿Qué le ocurre? | What's the trouble? |
| ¿Dónde le duele? | Where does it hurt? |
| ¿Cuánto tiempo hace que tiene usted este dolor? | How long have you had this pain? |
| ¿Cuánto tiempo lleva usted sintiéndose así? | How long have you been feeling like this? |
| Súbase la manga. | Roll up your sleeve. |
| Desvístase (hasta la cintura), por favor. | Please undress (down to the waist). |
| Quítese los pantalones y los calzoncillos. | Please remove your trousers and underpants. |

## PATIENT

| I feel... | Me siento... | may syayntoa |
|---|---|---|
| faint | desmayar | daysmahyahr |
| dizzy | mareado | mahrerahdhoa |
| nauseous | con náuseas | kon nowssehahss |
| shivery | con escalofríos | kon ayskahloafreeoass |

| I've/He's/She's got (a/an)... | Tengo/El tiene/Ella tiene... | tayngoa/ayl tyaynay/ aylyah tyaynay |
|---|---|---|
| abscess | un flemón | oon flehmon |
| asthma | asma | ahsmah |
| boil | un furúnculo | oon fooroonkooloa |
| chill | un enfriamiento | oon aynfreeahmyayntoa |
| cold | un constipado | oon koansteepahdhoa |
| cramps | calambre | kahlahmbray |
| diarrhoea | diarrea | dyahrrehah |
| fever | fiebre | fyehbray |
| haemorrhoids | hemorroides | aymoarroeedhayss |
| hay fever | fiebre del heno | fyehbray dayl aynoa |
| hernia | hernia | ehrnyah |

## DOCTOR

| Echese ahí, por favor. | Please lie down over there. |
|---|---|
| Abra usted la boca. | Open your mouth. |
| Respire hondo. | Breathe deeply. |
| Tosa usted, por favor. | Cough, please. |
| Le tomaré la temperatura. | I'll take your temperature. |
| Voy a tomarle la presión sanguínea. | I'm going to take your blood pressure. |
| ¿Es la primera vez que tiene esto? | Is this the first time you've had this? |
| Le pondré una inyección. | I'll give you an injection. |
| Quiero una muestra de su orina (sus heces). | I want a sample of your urine (stools). |

## PATIENT

| | | |
|---|---|---|
| indigestion | indigestión | eendeekhaystyon |
| inflammation of... | una inflamación de... | oonah eenflahmahthyon day |
| influenza | gripe | greepay |
| morning sickness | vómitos por la mañana | boameetoass por lah mahñahnah |
| rheumatism | reumatismo | rayoomahteesmoa |
| stiff neck | tortícolis | torteekoaleess |
| sunburn | quemaduras del sol | kaymahdhoorahss dayl sol |
| sunstroke | una insolación | oonah eensoalahthyon |
| ulcer | una úlcera | oonah oolthehrah |
| whooping cough | tos de pecho | toss day pehchoa |
| It's nothing serious, I hope? | Espero que no sea nada serio. | ayspehroa kay noa sehah nahdhah sehryoa |
| I'd like you to prescribe some medicine for me. | Me gustaría que me recetara alguna medicina. | may goostahreeah kay may raythaytahrah ahlgoonah maydeetheenah |

## DOCTOR

| | |
|---|---|
| No es nada como para preocuparse. | It's nothing to worry about. |
| Debe quedarse en cama durante... días. | You must stay in bed for... days. |
| Usted tiene... | You've got... |
| apendicitis | an appendicitis |
| artritis | arthritis |
| gripe | influenza |
| neumonía | pneumonia |
| un resfriado | a cold |
| Usted está agotado. Necesita un descanso. | You're over-tired. You need a rest. |
| Quiero que vaya usted al hospital para un reconocimiento general. | I want you to go to the hospital for a general check-up. |
| Le recetaré un antibiótico. | I'll prescribe an antibiotic. |

## PATIENT

| | | |
|---|---|---|
| I'm a diabetic. | **Soy diabético.** | soy dyah**bhay**teekoa |
| I've a cardiac condition. | **Sufro algo del corazón.** | soofroa ahlgoa dayl koarah**thon** |
| I had a heart attack in... | **Tuve un ataque al corazón en...** | too**bhay** oon ah**tah**kay ahl koarah**thon** ayn |
| I'm allergic to... | **Soy alérgico a...** | soy ah**lehr**kheekoa ah |
| This is my usual medicine. | **Esta es la medicina que tomo normalmente.** | aystah ayss lah maydee**thee**nah kay **toa**moa noarmahl**mayn**tay |
| I need this medicine. | **Necesito esta medicina.** | naythay**ssee**toa aystah maydee**thee**nah |
| I'm expecting a baby. | **Estoy esperando un bebé.** | aystoy ayspay**rahn**doa oon behbheh |
| Can I travel? | **¿Puedo viajar?** | pwaydhoa byahkhahr |

## DOCTOR

| | |
|---|---|
| **¿Qué dosis de insulina está usted tomando?** | What dosage of insulin are you taking? |
| **¿En inyección u oral?** | Injection or oral? |
| **¿Qué tratamiento ha estado siguiendo?** | What treatment have you been having? |
| **¿Qué medicina ha estado tomando?** | What medicine have you been having? |
| **Usted ha tenido un (ligero) ataque al corazón.** | You've had a (slight) heart attack. |
| **No utilizamos... en España. Esto es muy parecido.** | We don't use ... in Spain. This is very similar. |
| **¿Cuándo espera el niño?** | When is the baby due? |
| **Usted no puede viajar sino hasta...** | You can't travel until... |

# PATIENT

## Part 2—Wounds

| Could you have a look at this...? | ¿Podría examinar...? | poadreeah ayksahmeenahr |
|---|---|---|
| blister | esta ampolla | aystah ahmpoalyah |
| boil | este forúnculo | aystay foaroonkoaloa |
| bruise | este cardenal | aystay kahrdaynahl |
| burn | esta quemadura | aystah kaymahdhoorah |
| cut | esta cortadura | aystay koartahdhoorah |
| graze | este arañazo | aysta ahrahñahthoa |
| insect bite | esta picadura de insecto | aystah peekahdhoorah day eensehktoa |
| lump | este bulto | aystay booltoa |
| rash | este salpullido | aystay sahlpoolyeedhoa |
| sting | esta picadura | aystah peekahdhoorah |
| swelling | esta hinchazón | aystah eenchahthon |
| wound | esta herida | aystah ayreedhah |
| I can't move my... It hurts. | No puedo mover el/ la... Me duele. | noa pwaydhoa moabhehr ayl/lah... may dwaylay |

## DOCTOR

## Heridas

| (No) está infectado. | It's (not) infected. |
|---|---|
| Tiene una vértebra desgastada. | You've got a slipped disc. |
| Quiero que le hagan una radiografía. | I want you to have an X-ray. |
| Está... | It's... |
| roto/torcido dislocado/desgarrado | broken/sprained dislocated/torn |
| Se ha distensionado un músculo. | You've pulled a muscle. |
| Le daré un antiséptico. | I'll give you an antiseptic. |
| No es nada serio. | It's nothing serious. |
| Quiero que venga a verme dentro de ... días. | I want you to come and see me in... days' time. |

DOCTOR

## PATIENT

### Part 3—Nervous tension

| | | |
|---|---|---|
| I'm in a nervous state. | **Estoy muy nervioso.** | aystoy mwee nehrbyoassoa |
| I'm feeling depressed. | **Me siento deprimido.** | may syayntoa daypreemeedhoa |
| I want some sleeping pills. | **Quiero un somnífero.** | kyayroa oon somneefayroa |
| I can't eat/I can't sleep. | **No puedo comer/ No puedo dormir.** | noa pwaydhoa koamehr/ noa pwaydhoa dormeer |
| I'm having nightmares. | **Tengo pesadillas.** | tayngoa payssahdheelyahss |
| Can you prescribe a...? | **¿Puede recetarme un...?** | pwaydhay rehthaytahrmay oon |
| tranquilizer anti-depressant sedative | **tranquilizante anti-depresivo sedante** | trahnkeeleethahntay ahntee daypraysseebhoa saydhahntay |

## DOCTOR

### Tensión nerviosa

| | |
|---|---|
| **Usted sufre de tensión nerviosa.** | You're suffering from nervous tension. |
| **Usted necesita un descanso.** | You need a rest. |
| **¿Qué píldoras ha estado tomando?** | What pills have you been taking? |
| **¿Cuántas diarias?** | How many a day? |
| **¿Cuánto tiempo lleva usted sintiéndose así?** | How long have you been feeling like this? |
| **Le recetaré unas píldoras.** | I'll prescribe some pills. |
| **Le daré un sedante.** | I'll give you a sedative. |

## PATIENT

### Prescriptions and dosage

| | | |
|---|---|---|
| What kind of medicine is this? | ¿Qué clase de medicina es ésta? | kay **klahssay** day may-**dheetheenah** ayss **aystah** |
| How many times a day should I take it? | ¿Cuántas veces al día debo tomarla? | **kwahntahss baythayss** ahl **deeah daybhoa toamahrlah** |
| Must I swallow them whole? | ¿Debo tragármelas enteras? | **daybhoa trahgahrmaylahss ayntayrahss** |

### Fee

| | | |
|---|---|---|
| How much do I owe you? | ¿Qué le debo? | kay lay **daybhoa** |
| Do I pay you now or will you send me your bill? | ¿Le pago ahora o me va usted a mandar la cuenta? | lay **pahgoa ahorah** oa may bah **oostaydh** ah **mahndahr** lah **kwayntah** |
| Thanks for your help, Doctor. | Muchas gracias por todo, doctor. | **moochahss grahthyahss** por **toadhoa doaktor** |

## DOCTOR

### Recetas y dosis

Tome... cucharaditas de esta medicina cada... horas.

Take... teaspoons of this medicine every... hours.

Tome... píldoras con un vaso de agua...

Take... pills with a glass of water...

... veces al día
antes de cada comida
después de cada comida
por las mañanas
por la noche

... times a day
before each meal
after each meal
in the mornings
at night

### Honorarios

Son 500 pesetas, por favor.

That's 500 pesetas, please.

Págueme ahora, por favor.

Please pay me now.

Le mandaré la cuenta.

I'll send you a bill.

FOR NUMBERS, see page 175

DOCTOR

## Dentist

| | | |
|---|---|---|
| Can you recommend a good dentist? | **¿Puede recomendarme un buen dentista?** | pwaydhay rehkoamayndahrmay oon bwayn daynteestah |
| Can I make an (urgent) appointment to see Dr...? | **¿Puedo pedir cita (urgente) para ver al Doctor...?** | pwaydhoa paydheer theetah (oorkhayntay) pahrah behr ahl doaktor |
| Can't you possibly make it earlier than that? | **¿No sería posible antes?** | noa sayreeah poasseeblay ahntayss |
| I've a toothache. | **Tengo dolor de muelas.** | tayngoa doalor day mwaylahss |
| I've an abscess. | **Tengo un flemón.** | tayngoa oon flaymon |
| This tooth hurts. | **Me duele este diente.** | may dwaylay aystay dyayntay |
| at the top | **arriba** | ahrreebhah |
| at the bottom | **abajo** | ahbhahkhoa |
| in the front | **delante** | daylahntay |
| at the back | **detrás** | daytrahss |
| Can you fix it temporarily? | **¿Puede usted arreglarlo temporalmente?** | pwaydhay oostaydh ahrrehglahrloa taympoarahlmayntay |
| I don't want it extracted. | **No quiero que me la saque.** | noa kyayroa kay mah lah sahkay |
| I've lost a filling. | **He perdido un empaste.** | ay pehrdeedhoa oon aympahstay |
| The gum is very sore. | **Las encías están muy inflamadas.** | lahss ayntheeahss aystahn mwee eenflahmahdhahss |
| The gum is bleeding. | **Las encías sangran.** | lahss ayntheeahss sahngrahn |

## Dentures

| | | |
|---|---|---|
| I've broken this denture. | **Se me ha roto la dentadura.** | say may ah roatoa lah dayntahdhoorah |
| Can you repair this denture? | **¿Puede usted arreglar esta dentadura?** | pwaydhay oostaydh ahrrehglahr aystah dayntahdhoorah |
| When will it be ready? | **¿Cuándo estará hecha?** | kwahndhoa aystahrah aychah |

## Optician

| I've broken my glasses. | **Se me han roto las gafas.** | say may ahn **roa**toa lahss **gah**fahss |
| Can you repair them for me? | **¿Me las puede usted arreglar?** | may lahss **pway**dhay oostaydh ahrreh**glahr** |
| When will they be ready? | **¿Cuándo estarán listas?** | **kwahn**dhoa aysta**rahn** **lees**tahss |
| Can you change the lenses? | **¿Puede cambiar los lentes?** | **pway**dhay kahm**byahr** loss **layn**tayss |
| I want tinted lenses. | **Quiero cristales ahumados.** | **kyay**roa krees**tah**layss owmah**dhoass** |
| I want some contact lenses. | **Quiero lentes de contacto.** | **kyay**roa **layn**tayss day kon**tahk**toa |
| I'd like to buy a pair of binoculars. | **Quisiera comprar unos binoculares.** | kees**syay**rah kom**prahr** **oo**noass beenoakoo**lah**rayss |
| I'd like to buy a pair of sun-glasses. | **Quisiera comprar unas gafas de sol.** | kees**syay**rah kom**prahr** **oo**nahss **gah**fass day sol |
| How much do I owe you? | **¿Cuánto le debo?** | **kwahn**toa lay **day**bhoa |
| Do I pay you now or will you send me your bill? | **¿Le pago ahora o me manda una factura?** | lay **pah**goa ah**oh**rah oa may **mahn**dah **oo**nah fahk**too**rah |

# Reference section

### Where do you come from?

Whether you're a born traveller or not, you're sure to meet people from all over the world once you get away from home. You may well make friends among them. This page will help you to explain where you're from, where you've been or where you're going.

| | | |
|---|---|---|
| Africa | **Africa** | ahfreekah |
| Algeria | **Algeria** | ahlkhayryah |
| Andorra | **Andorra** | ahndorrah |
| Asia | **Asia** | ahssyah |
| Australia | **Australia** | owstrahlyah |
| Canada | **Canadá** | kahnahdhah |
| Central America | **América Central** | ahmayreekah thayntrahl |
| China | **China** | cheenah |
| England | **Inglaterra** | eenglahtehrrah |
| Europe | **Europa** | ayooroapah |
| France | **Francia** | frahnthyah |
| Germany | **Alemania** | ahlaymahnyah |
| Gibraltar | **Gibraltar** | kheebrahltahr |
| Great Britain | **Gran Bretaña** | grahn braytahñah |
| Ireland | **Irlanda** | eerlahndah |
| Italy | **Italia** | eetahlyah |
| Japan | **Japón** | khahpon |
| Morocco | **Marruecos** | mahrrwaykoass |
| New Zealand | **Nueva Zelandia** | nwaybhah zaylahndyah |
| North America | **América del Norte** | ahmayreekah dayl nortay |
| Portugal | **Portugal** | portoogahl |
| Scandinavia | **Escandinavia** | ayskahndeenahbhyah |
| Scotland | **Escocia** | ayskoathyah |
| South Africa | **Africa del Sur** | ahfreekah dayl soor |
| South America | **América del Sur** | ahmayreekah dayl soor |
| Spain | **España** | ayspahñah |
| Switzerland | **Suiza** | sweethah |
| Tunisia | **Túnez** | toonayth |
| United States | **Estados Unidos** | aystahdhoass ooneedhoass |
| Soviet Union | **Unión Soviética** | oonyon soabhyayteekah |
| Wales | **País de Gales** | paheess day gahlayss |

## Numbers

| | | |
|---|---|---|
| 0 | cero | thayroa |
| 1 | uno | oonoa |
| 2 | dos | doss |
| 3 | tres | trayss |
| 4 | cuatro | kwahtroa |
| 5 | cinco | theenkoa |
| 6 | seis | sayss |
| 7 | siete | syaytay |
| 8 | ocho | oachoa |
| 9 | nueve | nwaybhay |
| 10 | diez | dyayth |
| 11 | once | onthay |
| 12 | doce | doathay |
| 13 | trece | traythay |
| 14 | catorce | kahtorthay |
| 15 | quince | keenthay |
| 16 | dieciséis | dyaytheessayss |
| 17 | diecisiete | dyaytheessyaytay |
| 18 | dieciocho | dyaytheeoachoa |
| 19 | diecinueve | dyaytheenwaybhay |
| 20 | veinte | bayntay |
| 21 | veintiuno | baynteeoonoa |
| 22 | veintidós | baynteedhoss |
| 23 | veintitrés | baynteetrayss |
| 24 | veinticuatro | baynteekwahtroa |
| 25 | veinticinco | baynteetheenkoa |
| 26 | veintiséis | baynteesayss |
| 27 | veintisiete | baynteessyaytay |
| 28 | veintiocho | baynteeoachoa |
| 29 | veintinueve | baynteenwaybhay |
| 30 | treinta | trayntah |
| 31 | treinta y uno | trayntah ee oonoa |
| 32 | treinta y dos | trayntah ee doss |
| 33 | treinta y tres | trayntah ee trayss |
| 40 | cuarenta | kwahrayntah |
| 41 | cuarenta y uno | kwahrayntah ee oonoa |
| 42 | cuarenta y dos | kwahrayntah ee doss |
| 43 | cuarenta y tres | kwahrayntah ee trayss |
| 50 | cincuenta | theenkwayntah |
| 51 | cincuenta y uno | theenkwayntah ee oonoa |
| 52 | cincuenta y dos | theenkwayntah ee doss |
| 53 | cincuenta y tres | theenkwayntah ee trayss |
| 60 | sesenta | sayssayntah |
| 61 | sesenta y uno | sayssayntah ee oonoa |
| 62 | sesenta y dos | sayssayntah ee doss |
| 63 | sesenta y tres | sayssayntah e trayss |

| | | |
|---|---|---|
| 70 | setenta | saytayntah |
| 71 | setenta y uno | saytayntah ee oonoa |
| 72 | setenta y dos | saytayntah ee doss |
| 73 | setenta y tres | saytayntah ee trayss |
| 80 | ochenta | oachayntah |
| 81 | ochenta y uno | oachayntah ee oonoa |
| 82 | ochenta y dos | oachayntah ee doss |
| 83 | ochenta y tres | oachayntah ee trayss |
| 90 | noventa | noabhayntah |
| 91 | noventa y uno | noabhayntah ee oonoa |
| 92 | noventa y dos | noabhayntah ee doss |
| 93 | noventa y tres | noabhayntah ee trayss |
| 100 | cien | thyayn |
| 101 | ciento uno | thyayntoa oonoa |
| 102 | ciento dos | thyayntoa doss |
| 110 | ciento diez | thyayntoa dyayth |
| 120 | ciento veinte | thyayntoa bayntay |
| 130 | ciento treinta | thyayntoa trayntah |
| 140 | ciento cuarenta | thyayntoa kwahrayntah |
| 150 | ciento cincuenta | thyayntoa theenkwayntah |
| 160 | ciento sesenta | thyayntoa sayssayntah |
| 170 | ciento setenta | thyayntoa saytayntah |
| 180 | ciento ochenta | thyayntoa oachayntah |
| 190 | ciento noventa | thyayntoa noabhayntah |
| 200 | doscientos | dosthyayntoass |
| 300 | trescientos | traysthyayntoass |
| 400 | cuatrocientos | kwahtroathyayntoass |
| 500 | quinientos | keenyayntoass |
| 600 | seiscientos | saysthyayntoass |
| 700 | setecientos | saytaythyayntoass |
| 800 | ochocientos | oachoathyayntoass |
| 900 | novecientos | noabhaythyayntoass |
| 1,000 | mil | meel |
| 1,100 | mil cien | meelthyayn |
| 1,200 | mil doscientos | meeldosthyayntoass |
| 2,000 | dos mil | dosmeel |
| 5,000 | cinco mil | theenkoameel |
| 10,000 | diez mil | dyaythmeel |
| 50,000 | cincuenta mil | theenkwayntahmeel |
| 100,000 | cien mil | thyaynmeel |
| 1,000.000 | un millón | oon meelyon |
| 1,000.000.000 | mil millones | meel meelyoanayss |

| | | |
|---|---|---|
| first | **primero** | preemehroa |
| second | **segundo** | saygoondoa |
| third | **tercero** | tehrthayroa |
| fourth | **cuarto** | kwahrtoa |
| fifth | **quinto** | keentoa |
| sixth | **sexto** | sehkstoa |
| seventh | **séptimo** | sehpteemoa |
| eighth | **octavo** | oaktahbhoa |
| ninth | **noveno** | noabhehnoa |
| tenth | **décimo** | daytheemoa |
| | | |
| once | **una vez** | oonah behth |
| twice | **dos veces** | doss behthayss |
| three times | **tres veces** | trayss behthayss |
| | | |
| a half | **una mitad** | oonah meetahdh |
| half a... | **medio...** | mehdhyoa |
| half of... | **la mitad de...** | lah meetahdh day |
| half (adj.) | **medio** | mehdhyoa |
| a quarter | **un cuarto** | oon kwahrtoa |
| one third | **un tercio** | oon tehrthyoa |
| a pair of | **un par de** | oon pahr day |
| a dozen | **una docena** | oonah dothehnah |
| | | |
| 1982 | **mil novecientos ochenta y dos** | meel noabhaythyayntoass oachayntah ee doss |
| 1983 | **mil novecientos ochenta y tres** | meel noabhaythyayntoass oachayntah ee trayss |
| 1984 | **mil novecientos ochenta y cuatro** | meel noabhaythyayntoass oachayntah ee kwahtroa |
| 1985 | **mil novecientos ochenta y cinco** | meel noabhaythyayntoass oachayntah ee theenkoa |

# Time

**las doce y cuarto**
(lahss **doathay** ee
kwahrtoa)

**la una y veinte**
(lah oonah ee bayntay)

**las dos y veinticinco**
(lahss doss ee bayntee-
theenkoa)

**las tres y media**
(lahss trayss ee
maydhyah)

**las cinco menos
veinticinco**
(lahss **theenkoa** maynoass
baynteetheenkoa)

**las seis menos
veinte**
(lahss sayss maynoass
bayntay)

**las siete menos
cuarto**
(lahss **syaytay**
maynoass kwahrtoa)

**las ocho menos diez**
(lahss **oachoa** may-
noass dyayth)

**las nueve menos
cinco**
(lahss **nwaybhay**
maynoass theenkoa)

**las diez**
(lahss dyayth)

**las once y cinco**
(lahss **oanthay** ee
theenkoa)

**las doce y diez**
(lahss **doathay** ee dyayth)

In ordinary conversation, time is expressed as above. However, official time uses a 24-hours clock which means that after noon hours are counted from 13 to 24. For instance, 13.15 would be 1.15 p.m for us. At midnight time returns to 0 so that 12.17 a.m. is written 0 h. 17.

## What time is it?

| | | |
|---|---|---|
| What time is it? | **¿Qué hora es?** | kay oarah ayss |
| It's... | **Es/Son...** | ayss/son |
| Excuse me. Can you tell me the time? | **Perdone. ¿Puede decirme la hora?** | pehrdoanay. pwaydhay daytheermay lah oarah |
| I'll meet you at... tomorrow. | **Nos encontraremos en... mañana.** | noss aynkoantrahraymoass ayn... mahñahnah |
| I'm sorry I'm late. | **Siento llegar tarde.** | syayntoa lyaygahr tahrday |
| At what time does... open? | **¿A qué hora abre...?** | ah kay oarah ahbray |
| At what time does... close? | **¿A qué hora cierra...?** | ah kay oarah thyayrrah |
| How long will it last? | **¿Cuánto dura?** | kwahntoa doorah |
| What time will it end? | **¿A qué hora termina?** | ah kay oarah tehrmeenah |
| At what time should I be there? | **¿A qué hora debo estar allí?** | ah kay oarah daybhoa aystahr ahlyee |
| At what time will you be there? | **¿A qué hora llegará usted allí?** | ah kay oarah lyaygahrah oostaydh ahlyee |
| Can I come...? | **¿Puedo venir...?** | pwaydhoa bayneer |
| at 8 o'clock/at 2.30 | **a las 8/a las 2 y media** | ah lahss 8/ah lahss 2 ee maydhyah |
| after/afterwards | **después** | dayspwayss |
| before | **antes** | ahntayss |
| early | **temprano** | taymprahnoa |
| half an hour | **media hora** | maydhyah oarah |
| hour | **hora** | oarah |
| in time | **a tiempo** | ah tyaympoa |
| late | **tarde** | tahrday |
| midnight | **medianoche** | maydhyahnoachay |
| minute | **minuto** | meenootoa |
| noon | **mediodía** | maydhyoadheeah |
| quarter of an hour | **cuarto de hora** | kwahrtoa day oarah |
| second | **segundo** | saygoondoa |

REFERENCE SECTION

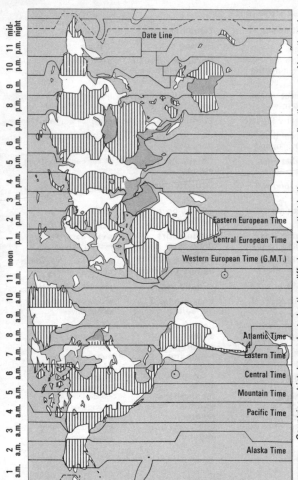

Countries which have adopted a time differing from that in the corresponding time zone. Note that also in the USSR, official time is one hour ahead of the time in each corresponding time zone. In summer, numerous countries advance time one hour ahead of standard time.

## Days

| What day is it today ? | ¿Qué día es hoy? | kay deeah ayss oy |
|---|---|---|
| Sunday | domingo | doameengoa |
| Monday | lunes | loonayss |
| Tuesday | martes | mahrtayss |
| Wednesday | miércoles | myayrkoalayss |
| Thursday | jueves | khwaybhayss |
| Friday | viernes | byayrnayss |
| Saturday | sábado | sahbhadhoa |

*Note:* The names of days and months aren't capitalized in Spanish.

| | | |
|---|---|---|
| in the morning | por la mañana | por lah mahñahnah |
| during the day | durante el día | doorahntay ayl deeah |
| in the afternoon | por la tarde | por lah tahrday |
| in the evening | por la tarde | por lah tahrday |
| at night | por la noche | por lah noachay |
| yesterday | ayer | ighehr |
| today | hoy | oy |
| tomorrow | mañana | mahñahnah |
| the day before | el día anterior | ayl deeah ahntehryor |
| the next day | el día siguiente | ayl deeah seegyayntay |
| two days ago | hace dos días | ahthay doss deeahss |
| in three days' time | en tres días | ayn trayss deeahss |
| last week | la semana pasada | lah saymahnah pahssahdhah |
| next week | la semana próxima | lah sahmahnah prokseemah |
| in two weeks | por una quincena | por oonah keenthehnah |
| birthday | el cumpleaños | ayl koomplayahñoass |
| day | el día | ayl deeah |
| day off | el día libre | ayl deeah leebray |
| holiday | el día festivo | ayl deeah faysteebhoa |
| holidays | las vacaciones | lahss bahkahthyonayss |
| month | el mes | ayl mayss |
| school holidays | las vacaciones del colegio | lahss bahkahthyonayss dayl koalehkhyoa |
| vacation | las vacaciones | lahss bahkahthyonayss |
| week | la semana | lah saymahnah |
| weekday | el día de la semana | ayl deeah day lah saymahnah |
| weekend | el fin de semana | ayl feen day saymahnah |
| working day | el día laborable | ayl deeah lahbhoarahblay |

## Months

| January | **enero** | aynayroa |
|---|---|---|
| February | **febrero** | fehbrehroa |
| March | **marzo** | mahrthoa |
| April | **abril** | ahbreel |
| May | **mayo** | mahyoa |
| June | **junio** | khoonyoa |
| July | **julio** | khoolyoa |
| August | **agosto** | ahgoastoa |
| September | **septiembre** | sehptyaymbray |
| October | **octubre** | oktoobray |
| November | **noviembre** | noabhyaymbray |
| December | **diciembre** | deethyaymbray |

| since June | **desde junio** | daysday khoonyoa |
|---|---|---|
| during the month of August | **durante el mes de agosto** | doorahntay ayl mayss day ahgoastoa |
| last month | **el mes pasado** | ayl mayss pahssahdhoa |
| next month | **el mes próximo** | ayl mayss prokseemoa |
| the month before | **el mes anterior** | ayl mayss ahntehryor |
| the month after | **el mes siguiente** | ayl mayss seegyayntay |
| July 1 | **el primero de julio** | ayl preemayroa day khoolyoa |
| March 17 | **el diecisiete de marzo** | ayl dyaytheessyaytay day mahrthoa |

Letter headings are written thus:

| Madrid, August 17, 19.. | **Madrid, 17 de agosto de 19..** |
|---|---|
| Barcelona, July 1, 19.. | **Barcelona, 1° de julio de 19..** |

## Seasons

| spring | **la primavera** | lah preemahbhehrah |
|---|---|---|
| summer | **el verano** | ayl bayrahnoa |
| autumn | **el otoño** | ayl otoañoa |
| winter | **el invierno** | ayl eenbyayrnoa |

| in spring | **en primavera** | ayn preemahbhehrah |
|---|---|---|
| during the summer | **durante el verano** | doorahntay ayl bayrahnoa |
| in autumn | **en otoño** | ayn otoañoa |
| during the winter | **durante el invierno** | doorahntay ayl eenbyayrnoa |

## Public holidays

These are the main public holidays in Spain when banks, offices and shops are closed. In addition, there are various regional holidays.

| | | |
|---|---|---|
| January 1 | **Año Nuevo** | New Year's Day |
| January 6 | **Epifanía** | Epiphany |
| March 19 | **San José** | St Joseph's Day |
| | **Viernes Santo** | Good Friday |
| | **Lunes de Pascua** | Easter Monday |
| May 1 | **Día del Trabajo** | Labour Day |
| | **Corpus Christi** | Corpus Christi Day |
| July 25 | **Santiago Apóstol** | St James's Day |
| August 15 | **Asunción** | Assumption Day |
| October 12 | **Día de la Hispanidad** | Columbus Day |
| November 1 | **Todos los Santos** | All Saints' Day |
| December 8 | **Inmaculada Concepción** | Immaculate Conception Day |
| December 25 | **Navidad** | Christmas Day |

## Seasonal temperatures

| | Málaga | Madrid | Barcelona | Pontevedra |
|---|---|---|---|---|
| January | 55°F | 40°F | 49°F | 47°F |
| April | 62 | 54 | 57 | 54 |
| July | 76 | 75 | 75 | 65 |
| October | 66 | 57 | 64 | 57 |

REFERENCE SECTION

## Abbreviations

| | | |
|---|---|---|
| A.C. | año de Cristo | A.D. |
| a/c | al cuidado de | c/o |
| a. de J.C. | antes de Jesucristo | B.C. |
| admon | administración | administration |
| apdo. | apartado de correos | post office box |
| Av., Avda. | Avenida | avenue |
| C., Cia. | Compañía | company |
| C/ | Calle | street, road |
| cta. | cuenta | account |
| cte. | corriente | of the present month |
| C.V. | caballos de vapor | horsepower |
| D. | Don | courtesy title (gentleman) |
| Da., Dª | Doña | courtesy title (lady) |
| EE.UU. | Estados Unidos | United States |
| f.c. | ferrocarril | railway |
| G.C. | Guardia Civil | police |
| h | hora | hour |
| h., hab. | habitantes | population |
| M.I.T. | Ministerio de Información y Turismo | Ministry of Information and Tourism |
| Nª Sª | Nuestra Señora | Our Lady, the Virgin |
| n.º, núm. | número | number |
| p. ej. | por ejemplo | for example |
| P. P. | porte pagado | postage paid |
| pta., ptas. | peseta(s) | peseta(s) |
| P.V.P. | precio de venta al público | retail price |
| R.A.C.E. | Real Automóvil Club de España | Royal Automobile Club of Spain |
| R.C. | Real Club... | Royal...Club |
| RENFE | Red Nacional de Ferrocarriles Españoles | Spanish National Railway |
| R.N.E. | Radio Nacional de España | Spanish National Broadcasting Company |
| S., Sta. | San, Santa | Saint |
| S.A. | Sociedad Anónima | Ltd., Inc. |
| Sr. | Señor | Mr. |
| Sra. | Señora | Mrs. |
| Sres., Srs. | Señores | gentlemen |
| Srta. | Señorita | Miss |
| TVE | Televisión Española | Spanish Television |
| Ud., Vd. | Usted | you (singular) |
| Uds., Vds. | Ustedes | you (plural) |
| v.g., v.gr. | verbigracia | viz., namely |

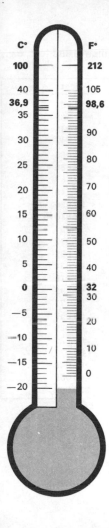

## Conversion tables

### Centimetres and inches

To change centimetres into inches, multiply by .39.

To change inches into centimetres, multiply by 2.54.

|        | in.   | feet  | yards |
|--------|-------|-------|-------|
| 1 mm   | 0,039 | 0,003 | 0,001 |
| 1 cm   | 0,39  | 0,03  | 0,01  |
| 1 dm   | 3,94  | 0,32  | 0,10  |
| 1 m    | 39,40 | 3,28  | 1,09  |

|        | mm    | cm    | m     |
|--------|-------|-------|-------|
| 1 in.  | 25,4  | 2,54  | 0,025 |
| 1 ft.  | 304,8 | 30,48 | 0,304 |
| 1 yd   | 914,4 | 91,44 | 0,914 |

(32 metres = 35 yards)

### Temperature

To convert Centigrade into degrees Fahrenheit, multiply Centigrade by 1.8 and add 32.

To convert degrees Fahrenheit into Centigrade, subtract 32 from Fahrenheit and divide by 1.8.

## Metres and feet

The figure in the middle stands for both metres and feet, e.g.,
1 metre = 3.281 ft. and 1 foot = 0.30 m.

| Metres | | Feet |
|---|---|---|
| 0.30 | 1 | 3.281 |
| 0.61 | 2 | 6.563 |
| 0.91 | 3 | 9.843 |
| 1.22 | 4 | 13.124 |
| 1.52 | 5 | 16.403 |
| 1.83 | 6 | 19.686 |
| 2.13 | 7 | 22.967 |
| 2.44 | 8 | 26.248 |
| 2.74 | 9 | 29.529 |
| 3.05 | 10 | 32.810 |
| 3.35 | 11 | 36.091 |
| 3.66 | 12 | 39.372 |
| 3.96 | 13 | 42.635 |
| 4.27 | 14 | 45.934 |
| 4.57 | 15 | 49.215 |
| 4.88 | 16 | 52.496 |
| 5.18 | 17 | 55.777 |
| 5.49 | 18 | 59.058 |
| 5.79 | 19 | 62.339 |
| 6.10 | 20 | 65.620 |
| 7.62 | 25 | 82.023 |
| 15.24 | 50 | 164.046 |
| 22.86 | 75 | 246.069 |
| 30.48 | 100 | 328.092 |

## Other conversion charts

REFERENCE SECTION

## Weight conversion

The figure in the middle stands for both kilograms and pounds, e.g., 1 kilogram = 2.205 1b. and 1 pound = 0.45 kilograms.

| Kilograms (kg.) | | Avoirdupois pounds |
|---|---|---|
| 0.45 | 1 | 2.205 |
| 0.90 | 2 | 4.405 |
| 1.35 | 3 | 6.614 |
| 1.80 | 4 | 8.818 |
| 2.25 | 5 | 11.023 |
| 2.70 | 6 | 13.227 |
| 3.15 | 7 | 15.432 |
| 3.60 | 8 | 17.636 |
| 4.05 | 9 | 19.840 |
| 4.50 | 10 | 22.045 |
| 6.75 | 15 | 33.068 |
| 9.00 | 20 | 44.889 |
| 11.25 | 25 | 55.113 |
| 22.50 | 50 | 110.225 |
| 33.75 | 75 | 165.338 |
| 45.00 | 100 | 220.450 |

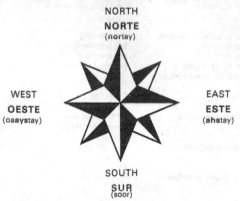

NORTH
**NORTE**
(nortay)

WEST
**OESTE**
(oaaystay)

EAST
**ESTE**
(ahstay)

SOUTH
**SUR**
(soor)

### What does that sign mean?

You may encounter some of the following signs or notices on your trip through Spain:

| | |
|---|---|
| Abierto | Open |
| Arriba | Up |
| Ascensor | Lift (elevator) |
| Caballeros | Gentlemen |
| Caja | Cashier |
| Caliente | Hot |
| Carretera particular | Private road |
| Cerrado | Closed |
| Cuidado | Caution |
| Cuidado con el perro | Beware of the dog |
| Debajo | Down |
| Empujar | Push |
| Entrada | Entrance |
| Frío (grifo) | Cold |
| Información | Information |
| Libre | Vacant |
| No obstruya la entrada | Do not block entrance |
| No tocar | Do not touch |
| Ocupado | Occupied |
| Peligro | Danger |
| Peligro de muerte | Danger of death |
| Permitido fumar | Smoking allowed |
| Privado | Private |
| ... prohibido | No... |
| Prohibido arrojar basuras | No littering |
| Prohibido entrar | No entrance |
| Prohibido fumar | No smoking |
| Prohibida la entrada a personas no autorizadas | No trespassing |
| Rebajas | Sale |
| Reservado | Reserved |
| Salida | Exit |
| Salida de emergencia | Emergency exit |
| Se alquila | To let (for rent) |
| Se vende | For sale |
| Sendero para bicicletas | Bicycle path |
| Señoras | Ladies |
| Tirar | Pull |
| Toque el timbre por favor | Please ring |

## Emergency

By the time the emergency is upon you, it's too late to turn to this page to find the Spanish for «I'll scream if you...». So have a look at this short list beforehand—and, if you want to be on the safe side, learn the expressions shown in capitals.

| | | |
|---|---|---|
| Be quick | **Sea rápido** | sehah rahpeedhoa |
| Call the police | **Llame a la policía** | lyahmay ah lah poalee-theeah |
| CAREFUL | **CUIDADO** | kweedhahdhoa |
| Come here | **Venga aquí** | bayngah ahkee |
| Come in | **Entre** | ayntray |
| Danger | **Peligro** | payleegroa |
| FIRE | **FUEGO** | fwaygoa |
| Gas | **Gas** | gahss |
| Get a doctor | **Busque un doctor** | booskay oon doaktor |
| Go away | **Váyase** | bahyahssay |
| HELP | **SOCORRO** | sokoarroa |
| Get help quickly | **Busque ayuda rápido** | booskay ahyoodhah rahpeedhoa |
| I'm ill | **Estoy enfermo** | aystoy ahnfehrmoa |
| I'm lost | **Me he perdido** | may ay payrdheedhoa |
| I've lost my... | **He perdido mi...** | ay payrdheedhoa mee |
| Keep your hands to yourself | **Guárdese sus manos** | gwahrdayssay sooss mahnoass |
| Leave me alone | **Déjeme en paz** | daykhaymay ayn pahth |
| Lie down | **Acuéstese** | ahkwaystayssay |
| Listen | **Escuche usted** | ayskoochay oostaydh |
| Listen to me | **Escúcheme usted** | ayskoochaymay oostaydh |
| Look | **Mire usted** | meeray oostaydh |
| Look out | **Cuidado** | kweedhahdhoa |
| POLICE | **POLICIA** | poaleetheeah |
| Quick | **Rápido** | rahpeedhoa |
| STOP | **DETENGASE** | daytayngahssay |
| Stop here | **Deténgase aquí** | daytayngahssay ahkee |
| Stop that man | **Detenga a ese hombre** | daytayngah ah ayssay oambray |
| Stop thief | **Al ladrón** | ahl lahdron |
| Stop or I'll scream | **Deténgase o grito** | daytayngahssay oa greetoa |

REFERENCE SECTION

FOR CAR ACCIDENTS, see page 150

# Index

## Quick reference page

Here are some phrases and expressions which you'll probably need most frequently on your trip:

| | | |
|---|---|---|
| Please. | **Por favor.** | por fah**bohr** |
| Thank you. | **Gracias.** | grah**thyahss** |
| Yes/No. | **Sí/No.** | see/noa |
| Excuse me. | **Perdone.** | pehr**doanay** |
| Waiter, please. | **Camarero, por favor.** | kahmah**rayroa** por fah**bhor** |
| How much is that? | **¿Cuánto es eso?** | **kwahntoa** ayss **ayssoa** |
| Where are the toilets? | **¿Dónde están los servicios?** | **doanday** ay**stahn** loss sehr**beethyoass** |

| **Lavabos** (lah**bhahbhoass**) | **Toilets** |
|---|---|
|  |  |
| **CABALLEROS** (kahbhah**lyayroass**) | **SEÑORAS** (say**ñoarahss**) |

| | | |
|---|---|---|
| Could you tell me...? | **¿Podría decirme...?** | poa**dreeah** day**theermay** |
| where/when/why | **dónde/cuándo/por qué** | **doanday**/**kwahndoa**/por kay |
| Help me, please. | **Ayúdeme, por favor.** | ah**yoodhaymay** por fah**bhor** |
| Where is the ... consulate? | **Dónde está el consulado...?** | **doanday** ay**stah** ayl koansoo**lahdoa** |
| American | **americano** | ahmayree**kahnoa** |
| British | **inglés** | een**glayss** |
| Canadian | **canadiense** | kahnahd**yaynsay** |
| What does this mean? I don't understand. | **¿Qué quiere decir esto? No lo entiendo.** | kay **kyayray** day**theer** **aystoa**? noa loa aynt**hyayndoa** |
| Do you speak English? | **¿Habla usted inglés?** | **ahblah** oo**staydh** een**glayss** |